James M. Greenwood

Principles of Education

Practically Applied

James M. Greenwood

Principles of Education

Practically Applied

ISBN/EAN: 9783337312633

Printed in Europe, USA, Canada, Australia, Japan

Cover: Foto ©Paul-Georg Meister /pixelio.de

More available books at **www.hansebooks.com**

PRINCIPLES OF EDUCATION

PRACTICALLY APPLIED

BY

J. M. GREENWOOD, A. M.

SUPERINTENDENT OF SCHOOLS, KANSAS CITY, MO.

NEW YORK
D. APPLETON AND COMPANY
1899

THE AUTHOR'S PREFACE.

THE motive that induced the author to submit this little volume for publication *is to help the teachers of this country to do better and more intelligent work in the school-room.*

It assumes that education is a science; that school-teachers can understand the principles of this science; and that in their daily work they can apply these principles with unerring certainty to the children under their control.

In the presentation of topics the teacher is told in plain language *what to do* as well as *what to avoid.* The directions are therefore simple, pointed, and emphatic.

The object of the work throughout is to impress this important question upon the mind of the teacher: "*How shall I teach so as to have my pupils become self-reliant, independent, manly men and womanly women?*"

J. M. GREENWOOD.

KANSAS CITY, MO.

CONTENTS.

CHAP.	PAGE
I.—THE APPLICATION OF THE PRINCIPLES OF PSYCHOLOGY TO THE WORK OF TEACHING	1
II.—SCHOOL MANAGEMENT	20
III.—PRINCIPLES OF CLASS MANAGEMENT	37
IV.—METHODS OF CONDUCTING RECITATIONS—DIRECTIONS TO PUPILS—DIRECTIONS TO TEACHERS	49
V.—LENGTH OF RECITATION	61
VI.—ART OF QUESTIONING	71
VII.—TEACHING READING	82
VIII.—TEACHING COMPOSITION AND LANGUAGE	98
IX.—TEACHING PENMANSHIP	114
X.—TEACHING GEOGRAPHY	128
XI.—TEACHING HISTORY	140
XII.—TEACHING ARITHMETIC	153
XIII.—HEALTH AND HYGIENE	165
XIV.—ONLY A BOY	173

PRINCIPLES OF EDUCATION PRACTICALLY APPLIED.

CHAPTER I.

THE APPLICATION OF THE PRINCIPLES OF PSYCHOLOGY TO THE WORK OF TEACHING.

This subject will be treated under three divisions:
I. *Temperaments.*
II. *Educational Psychology.*
III. *Educational Principles and their Application.*

It is assumed that the teacher must learn what to do, how to do, when to do, and when to leave off. Owing to the nature of his work, he deals chiefly with mind and its manifestations as made known through the body, and hence he is supposed to be familiar with the elements of psychology, and not unacquainted with the theory and art of teaching. Thus qualified, his success as a teacher hinges entirely upon the right application of the educational forces he uses in imparting instruction and in arousing self-activity in the minds of the learners. This gives a double phase to education—instruction and culture. The foregoing implies upon the part of the teacher a working knowledge of the human mind in general, its laws of growth, modes of action, and methods of culture; also, an intimate acquaintance with the physiologic, hygienic, and mental conditions of those to be taught, and the nature, influence, and limits of the means employed in conveying knowledge and awakening thought. The teacher, it is admitted, may be well read in psychology as an abstract science, and capable of talking intelligently upon any special department thereof, and yet fail in teaching, because of inability to adjust and to adapt his educational psychology to the capacity of his pupils. Owing to this fact, many intelligent and ·conscientious teachers, having worked earnestly and industriously, are puzzled in trying to understand why their efforts are so unproductive of substantial results. Perhaps some light may be thrown on this mystery.

As a class, teachers do not study child-mind understandingly. They begin the subject at the wrong end. What psychology the most of them know has been learned from books, and to nearly all of them it is a nebulous mass at best. Much of it, when put into the plainest language, needs to be translated or diluted before they know what it means. Right heartily do they "wish that writers on psychology would mix more organized common-sense with their metaphysics, and convey their ideas in simple words that common people can understand." Doubtless this is the reason why so many teachers have associated an intangible something —difficult to grasp and harder to retain—with the words "mental philosophy, psychology, and metaphysics." Turning away in disgust from a subject that yields so little, they fall back on experience and observation, and thus virtually deny that the scattered facts in methods of culture are susceptible of classification, and that any general principles may be deduced therefrom. From such premises, indeed, it is not strange that they fail to discover any relation between psychological principles and their application to living children; and, moreover, they are apt to look with distrust upon any statement affirming that such a relationship exists, and that it can be discovered and applied in teaching. Being unable to harmonize bookish psychology with the facts before them, they depart on divergent lines of thought and action in their school-work. Against nature, their pupils are mentally and physically forced so far as the educational machinery can crush and form them into the same molds. Instead of intelligent work, it is educational mechanism. Both teachers and school-officers need awakening on this subject. Child-mind must be studied in the children themselves. The child is the starting-point. Here the teacher must begin as an intelligent, patient observer, and watch carefully the unfolding of every faculty, its laws of growth and methods of culture. Books and lectures are helps not to be disparaged, yet they are not the only sources of knowledge. For instance, the boy who studies geology only from books may pick up some general notions in regard to that science, but put him out among the rocks and he is lost, helpless, and confused; and so it is in studying mind, divorced from living people. Naked mind we are not familiar with, and do not know how to treat it.

Let us attend, however, to a more practical phase of this subject, and one, too, that is neglected in nearly all the training-schools of this country, and yet it is, in my opinion, one of the most essential qualifications that the teacher can possess, namely, a critical knowledge of

I. THE HUMAN TEMPERAMENTS.

The brain is the organ, or instrument, that the mind uses in acquiring or in imparting knowledge; in other words, it is the organ of the mind, and the mind is manifested through the brain. Now, the human mind is so constituted that it groups objects that are alike together, and separates those that are unlike. This is the natural method, and it lies at the foundation of all logical classification as well as all progress in the various fields of human thought. A law that is so universal in its nature and so comprehensive in its details, and is alike applicable to individuals, species, genera, classes, and kingdoms, should not be neglected in the grand work of human culture. To give a more practical direction to these suggestions, let us consider briefly the object of our solicitude, *the child*, composed, according to the teachings of physiology, of three systems, consisting of ten apparatuses, forming thirty-nine different organs. This is the child as a material organism. This organism can exist only by complying with certain well-known conditions, and these are conditions of growth, which are proper food, clothing and shelter, exercise, rest, and sleep. For purposes of classification according to their functions, the three systems are the blood-producing, blood-circulating, and the nervous system.

At a glance, an experienced physiologist can tell which of these systems predominates in any particular person that may come before him or be accurately described to him; or he can balance with nice discrimination the relations that these systems bear to one another. Such knowledge is acquired by observation, experience, and reflection. In the art of healing, this knowledge is an essential element. Experienced stockmen will select from a large drove of cattle or horses those animals having peculiar qualities and dispositions. Those judges of animal nature seldom or never make mistakes. Vast differences exist in the fiber and structure of the various kinds of wood that lumber-men well understand. They know what strain or pressure each kind will sustain, and what weight it will support. Should the teacher's knowledge of those committed to his care be any the less accurate? Should it not be more so? True; but how can this precise knowledge be acquired? Answer: By the teachers' studying the temperaments of living people closely, carefully, and intelligently, until they can tell instantly the prevailing temperament or combination of temperaments of any child. Temperament determines the prevailing bias of disposition, whether natural or acquired, and upon it depends the sum total of our inclinations and prevailing tendencies. The temperaments are formed by the proportion of those elements that enter into the bodily structure, causing the diversities in shape, form, and mental characteristics that we observe; and whether we employ the words "lymphatic, sanguine, bilious, and nervous," or "vital, motive, and mental," to denote the bodily constitution of individuals, these terms correspond to those real distinctions which prompt the possessor to move or act in a certain direction. The mind is a unit; it manifests its activity in various directions. A distinct kind of mind activity is called a faculty of the mind; consequently, there are as many faculties of the mind as it has distinct kinds of activity. In like manner, the body is one organism, constructed upon temperamental conditions. The manner of their combination produces tendencies either to mental activity or to sluggishness, causing all those variations in human nature that we observe. When the intellect, sensibility, or will prevails, there is found a corresponding temperamental development which exerts a controlling influence, and shapes and colors the whole character of the possessor. He lives and acts in harmony with his nature. Teachers furnished with eyes, ears, good sense, and an inclination to study, can tell what tendencies prevail in the pupils they are called upon to teach. This is justly regarded as the key to eminent success.

The child in whom the nervous temperament predominates certainly requires different incentives, both in instruction and management, from the one whose strongest temperament is the bilious or sanguine, or a combination of them. It is not claimed that studying the temperaments is the same as studying mind; but the channels along which the mind's activity and intensity manifest themselves are legitimate subjects of investigation. Furthermore, the teacher who first prepares himself by a thorough working knowledge of the temperamental conditions of childhood is better equipped for discerning character and the various modes of treatment applicable to it than the one ignorant of these truths. Of all persons, the teacher should be the most deeply versed in the philosophy of the human mind. He should be familiar with mind in its higher as well as in its simpler forms. Mind in childhood, in its most elementary forms, he should know. A word or a smile to one child may be more repellant or attractive than a whipping or a valuable gift to another. A teacher who is a correct judge of human nature knows how to adapt instruction to the capacity of learners. From the very first day that the child of a highly-wrought nervous organization enters school, the intelligent teacher feels a deep solicitude for him, and advises much out-door recreation and frequent rests from study, early bedtime and refreshing sleep. The sturdy boy, having a compact organization, capacious lung power, and good digestion, needs to work off his superabundant energy in various directions. The school-house may be either a prison or a palace to him, depending upon how he is put into it and kept there. And just here we are brought face to face with one of the most serious questions connected with American civilization, namely, whether we are not developing too highly, in the school children of this country, the nervous system, and dwarfing the growth of the blood-producing and the blood-circulating systems. Information collected from numerous sources points in that direction, particularly in our cities and towns. As it is beyond the limits of the present discussion to pursue this phase of the subject further, reference to it in this connection serves the purpose of indicating the vast issues involved in the subject of education, and as influencing the physical characteristics of our people. This is a serious question that educators must meet.

Not only should the teacher be able to tell at sight what temperament predominates in any particular child, but also what temperament prevails in his own organization, and its combining ratios with the other temperaments. Knowing himself, he can institute a series of comparisons between himself and others, and possibly this may be the means of correcting some of his own faults. It is a well-established fact that the temperamental condition of a person may be somewhat modified in a series of years. The teacher, by vigilant effort, is able in time to tame the young barbarian into an intelligent, refined, and cultured gentleman. Nervous children, if placed under a calm, quiet, self-possessed teacher, one that does not fret and worry and fidget, will become steady; he will teach them to avoid many excitants that would otherwise strain their nerves to the highest pitch. The teacher who can not adapt himself to his pupils, and who fails to acquire a firm grasp on their affections by holding in check the vicious tendencies and unfolding the better ones, will not succeed in making them useful and honorable members of society.

II. Educational Psychology.

Education is not a matter of chance. It is an orderly development of man's powers, that furnishes his mind with knowledge, and gives him skill to use it. All growth proceeds in accordance with some regular plan of development. This plan is the law. All plants and animals grow according to laws governing their lives. They grow under certain conditions, and, if these conditions are not supplied, death ensues. Law is written everywhere and in the plainest characters. Proper soil, heat, moisture, and light, the plant must have, or it withers and dies. The wild bird, imprisoned in the cage, frets and struggles and dies—dies trying to free itself. Plant-life symbolizes human growth and culture; yet the educational life of the child as far transcends that of the mere plant as human intelligence rises in grandeur above the life-principle imbedded in the kernel of grain. Education as a science is based upon fundamental principles, which express the laws of human life and its development. The highest interpretation that we can give to this conception is the perfection of the individual for the duties of life.

The child is the central figure in all educational systems. His powers are multiplex, and his possibilities infinite; the former may be unfolded in their natural order by the skillful teacher, while he can only direct the latter by inspiring to lofty endeavor. ✓Thus the teacher is the molder, builder, and architect of his own school. As his conception of education grows and expands daily, so will his workmanship become more perfect and symmetrical. Such high trusts demand consummate skill, rare tact, cultivated taste, and unerring judgment. Earnest, diligent, enthusiastic, and soul-inspiring, the true teacher is always a learner. All possibilities of the race he recognizes as latent in the child. When the child is charged, can the teacher draw out the sparks? This human machine may contain a concentration of pointed and startling traits of character transmitted for a dozen generations. Herein lies another difficult question, and one which embarrasses thousands of teachers. No account is taken of hereditary tendencies. Presuming that the ponderous school-mill will grind out about the same quantity and quality of flour, however great the variety may be in the grain furnished, teachers are too frequently forgetful that blind forces, working upon sensitive minds, may blight and mildew the fairest hopes and the brightest prospects—may cause the most active minds to stagnate. Teachers at the beginning of school should acquaint themselves with all the essential factors and tendencies of each pupil. Such information simplifies school management, and effectually disposes of "that very peculiar boy" who rules the household and is so annoying to his teacher. In possession of such facts, the teacher would enter upon his work intelligently. There may be twenty different factors in a pupil's nature that the teacher ought to know, but, being ignorant of them, a system of guess-work is adopted, with the usual well-known results!

It is no unusual thing in "school-keeping," as it is called, to find the "keeper" ignorant of the nature, habits, associations, and dispositions of the pupils attending his school. Every child is a problem to be studied, interpreted, and understood aright. A mere lad is not qualified to preside as judge in our civil or criminal courts to mete out justice to the people. The judge is a man learned, or supposed to be learned, in the law. The minister, whose calling is a high and sacred one, must keep abreast of those vital issues which bear directly upon man's present and future happiness. How much more important, then, is it that the teacher should have that professional knowledge that study and experience only can give! The teacher, owing to the relation that he sustains to his pupils, is judge, physician, minister, and teacher, all centered in one individual. These sacred trusts are committed to his keeping. Should he cease to improve or to grow in knowledge and wisdom, they will perish in his hands. To stand still is death; only growth is life.

III. Educational Principles.

1. To grow is a law of our being.
2. The mind is self-active.
3. Body and mind are interdependent, and must be studied together.
4. The teacher must know the nature of childhood and the laws of human development.
5. The teacher should understand the order in which the faculties of the human mind are unfolded.
6. This knowledge can be acquired by studying body and mind and their phenomena.
7. Education is a growth, and is effected by thought and the expression of thought.
8. In teaching, the matter and the method must be adapted to the capacity of the learner.
9. The teacher must know the subject-matter to be taught, and its relations to other subjects.
10. Attention on the part of the learner is the condition of acquiring knowledge.
11. In teaching, the learner must pass by easy steps from the *known* to the *unknown*.
12. The concrete phase of a subject should precede the abstract, and the objective should precede the subjective.
13. Only one thing should be taught at a time, and the learner's understanding should be thoroughly reached.
14. All intellectual progress depends upon the learner's ability to discern agreements and differences.
15. The teacher stimulates and directs the learner, but all education comes from the learner's voluntary effort.

16. "The highest perfection of the individual is the true object of education."

The foregoing principles are based upon the science of human development. Some of them refer to the learner, others to the teacher, and others again to learner and teacher. Those referring to methods may be employed in teaching any of the common or higher branches, and at any stage of the learner's progress. No restrictions are imposed on any of them save the limits of the teacher's ingenuity to devise illustrations. Educational principles are guide-posts that say: "This way, sir!" When the teacher departs from them he travels over rough and thorny roads, and is kept retracing his steps, hardly making any progress. When the blind lead the blind, there is no one to watch for the ditch, and, when they tumble into it, there is no hand near to help them out. The word "struggling" well represents most of the work in our schools. Struggling teachers, struggling children — all strugglers! How we long to lift them out and set them traveling on smooth roads and face foremost! Struggling with words, rules, tables, and definitions, appears to be the end and glory for which school children live and suffer.

Some illustrations will now be adduced from methods of teaching arithmetic. The following are selected from an arithmetic just published, and will serve the purpose of illustrating one phase of this subject. The pupil is directed to copy and complete the following and other exercises:

$$4 + 2 = ?, \quad 5 + 2 = ?, \quad 5 - 2 = ?,$$
$$7 + 3 = ?, \quad 2 + 5 = ?, \quad 3 - 2 = ?,$$
$$6 - 2 = ?, \quad 3 + 8 = ?, \quad \text{etc.}$$

PRINCIPLES OF PSYCHOLOGY IN TEACHING. 13

It is evident that such exercises possess some genuine merit, yet they make a very thin mental diet. Let us take the equation $4 + 2 = ?$, and examine it. Putting four and two together is one act of the mind—a synthesis—and so of the other expressions of like form. Again $5 - 2 = ?$, involves an additional element—analysis—and is one step in advance. When once the child has learned that four and two are six, a thousand repetitions will give him no new information, and it is a waste of time to keep him employed in that manner. Suppose, however, that we put this equation under another form and less restricted, the figure "6" may then assume a new meaning. Suppose we request the class to find all the numbers by adding two at a time that will make "6" At once they are set thinking, and each one must think for himself. The number "6" is broken to pieces, the parts examined, and put together again. Genuine sparks of thought fly about the number "6" as the little hands are raised in token of results. Here are the results in full, using integers only:

Operation.—$4 + 2 = 6$, $3 + 3 = 6$, $5 + 1 = 6$, $6 + 0 = 6$. The child sees "6" under all these forms. Having drilled on a few numbers, the work may be extended by adding three numbers at a time to make "6."

Operation.—$4 + 1 + 1 = 6$, $3 + 2 + 1 = 6$, $2 + 2 + 2 = 6$, $5 + 1 + 0 = 6$, $6 + 0 + 0 = 6$.

Such exercises may be indefinitely extended, followed immediately by taking numbers together and apart. Given $4 + ? - ? = 6$. Here the missing numbers are to be supplied, or as many of them as time will permit.

$$\text{Operation.} — 4 + 3 - 1 = 6.$$
$$4 + 4 - 2 = 6.$$
$$4 + 5 - 3 = 6.$$
$$4 + 6 - 4 = 6.$$
$$\text{etc.}$$

By a slight change we have $? + ? - ? + 2 = 6$, and again the learner may start in pursuit of results. It is now evident that these and similar exercises may be extended till the signs of multiplication and division are employed, and fractional numbers are used with the same facility as integers. Such exercises require clear, concise, intelligent thought-work, and stand in striking contrast to dull mechanical drudgery: that only stagnates and does not educate.

Again, a class is to learn the "Table of Long Measure." How shall they learn it? Committing the "table" to memory by repeating it over and over till all "can say it," is the universal method. This method is an outrage, an insult, an irreparable injury to the children. It violates every educational principle, except one prevalent in China. To verify a table is the rational manner of learning it. Each pupil should be provided with a foot-ruler, and set to work measuring such objects in the school-room as the teacher may designate. The arbitrary length, the inch, is marked off, and from it the learner gets his first definite conception of measured distance. Counting the inches in a foot, the unit of measure is fixed in his mind. In measuring, care must be taken that it is done correctly. By short steps the learner goes from the foot to the yard, from the yard to the rod, and, by reversing the steps, back again to inches. Having measured different objects in the school-room, a wider field of objects may be selected about the school grounds. Pertinent questions by the teacher, addressed to the pupils as the work progresses, will fix the facts firmly in each mind. In every act of measurement the pupil uses analysis and synthesis—*reduction ascending* and *reduction descending*. Mentally, he passes rapidly up and down the scale. The foot-ruler is to be followed by using the yard-stick and tape-line in measuring objects of considerable length. Such practical work cultivates the eye, hand, observation, attention, judgment, and reason, and the pupil retains what he learns.

As another exercise, " Wine Measure " may be presented. The school should be furnished with a gill, a pint, a quart, and a gallon measure; also with a bucket of water, or a bushel or two of sand. Everything in readiness, a member of the class will dip up a gill of whatever is to be measured and empty it into the pint cup, and repeat till this vessel is filled, and it in turn emptied into the quart cup, the class noting particularly the number of gills in a pint, and also in a quart. Now the gill, pint, or quart measure may be used to fill the gallon vessel or to empty it. The children, keeping account of the gills, pints, and quarts in a gallon, understand every step in the process, and know the why and wherefore. The table means something, and they can explain the meaning. *Doing* is the way to *knowing*, and this is the fact emphasized. What is true of these two "tables" is correspondingly true of other tables of weights and measures. Thousands of children can repeat glibly " Avoirdupois Weight," yet they can not weigh a pound of butter on the scales.

Shall we not bridge this great chasm between school work and the practical duties of life?

The world's great teachers are most valuable to us, not on account of the discoveries they have made, but on account of the power they have given us to get knowledge for ourselves, and the mental activity they inspire. Hence one of the great objects in teaching is to put the learner in such a position that he must get knowledge for himself, and follow his own inclination doing so; yet his efforts should be directed by the teacher. To keep abreast of his work, the teacher is required to analyze his subjects and frequently to reconstruct them, and to devote his attention to the learner's mind. Thoroughly conversant with his subjects and well grounded in the principles of human nature, he is properly qualified to impart instruction and to manage children successfully. He is able also to trace the proper connection of *what* he teaches and *how* he teaches with the fundamental operations of the human mind as related to the body and acting through the nerves, muscles, and special senses. Intellectual acts he distinguishes as belonging to two classes—the perception of agreements and the perception of differences, supplemented by memory, or the power to hold in the mind what has once been perceived. The power of observing differences is, perhaps, more important in an educational sense than that of noting agreements, although they are the complements of each other. Differences strike us everywhere. By differences persons and things are separated and regarded as distinct. Complete knowledge unites in thought what an object is, by separating it from what it is not. Agreements form classes, and individual objects picked out of classes make differences. The unskillful teacher relies almost entirely upon teaching agreements and neglecting differences. Such instruction is one-sided, narrow, and superficial.

Certain operations of the mind take place in the acquisition of knowledge. The several steps in the process are so clearly established that all thinking persons accept them. Analyzing a mental operation by which an object of thought is reached and fixed in the mind, the steps appear as follow:

1. Attention; 2. Abstraction; 3. Analysis; 4. Synthesis; 5. Comparison; 6. Identification; 7. Discrimination; 8. Classification.

To obtain these results, it is the teacher's duty to stick closely to the point under consideration. Instead of spading around in the neighborhood of any particular topic, he digs it up root and branch, and holds it before the minds of his class till they grasp it with a power that never relaxes. By appropriation and assimilation it becomes their own.

Another important distinction, but most unfortunately lost sight of in teaching, is in not distinguishing sharply between thought and the expression of thought. Thought naturally precedes expression. Thought appears to spring up instantly in the mind, while the expression is of slower growth. Ideas go before words. Words symbolize ideas, that others may grasp the thought they are intended to express. Therefore, education is composed of two complementary parts—thought and the expression of thought. It is important in all cases for the teacher to know whether any difficulty that a pupil may have in learning is owing to an error in thought or to a defect in expression. If an error exist in thought, it can not be corrected by correcting the language. The source of error is deeper than any verbal distinction, hence the necessity for deciding correctly to which the error belongs. A learner may use language well, apparently, yet be incapable of thinking either correctly or vigorously. No amount of language drill will cause him to improve his forms of thought, and neither will thought-work always improve or cultivate the power of expressing ideas clearly, forcibly, and elegantly. Dimness of thought, or failure to grasp an idea firmly and to hold it tenaciously, may be the weak point in the pupil's mind. To remove dimness of thought, repeated explanations and demonstrations are necessary. Defects in expression are remedied by constant and careful practice in the choice of language, which should be a prominent feature of every recitation. The uppermost question in actual school work is the form of thought and how to express it. The ability to do stalwart thinking is one of the lost arts in most schools. The general drift is setting strongly to memorizing. Memorizing rules, definitions, "beautiful sentiments," and a vast amount of gilt-edged rubbish and padding, that have no educational significance, except as clogs to thought and leaden feet to progress. Awkwardly the boy may express his ideas, and with difficulty make himself understood; yet this awkward boy may think well, and in time acquire an easy, natural, and graceful style of expression. Rob him of his thoughts, and his language betrays his ignorance. Education rests upon the thought-basis as its pivotal center.

Thought has life, activity, growth in it. Memory is the form of education minus the soul. It is the receiving vault in which thought is imprisoned, and then starved to death.

CHAPTER II.

SCHOOL MANAGEMENT.

In discussing school management we aim to ascertain the best methods of conducting all the affairs of a school. The particular points to be considered are, first, the school-house; secondly, the organization of classes; thirdly, the movements of classes; and fourthly, the daily programme of exercises.

The construction of a school-building may aid the teacher very materially in the management of the school, or it may be so inconvenient and so poorly adapted to school purposes as to subvert many things that should be accomplished in school work.

In this discussion my remarks are intended to apply to country schools as well as to city and town graded schools. Nearly seven tenths of all the children in the nation must be educated in the country schools. These schools are the people's colleges. The remaining three tenths are educated in private and graded schools. Most of the States have systems of schools, and, though not alike in all respects, the following general classification will apply to most of them.

Under a State system of schools there are, first, the ungraded and graded elementary schools; secondly—a step higher—the high schools, academies, and seminaries; and thirdly—still another step higher—the normal schools for the training of teachers. Besides these, there are, in many of the States, universities for a still more advanced course of study, and many private schools and colleges. This simple classification will show what is meant by a State system, though the organization in many of the States is as yet very imperfect.

School-houses and their location. In some of the country districts the school-house is to be found in one of the most inaccessible places in the district. It is a matter of considerable importance where the school-house in a district is located. It should be central, so that children from all parts of the district can easily get to it. The grounds about it should be desirable and inviting as well as convenient, and should be selected with a view to the interests of the children rather than to those of some one who wishes to give an acre of land which he can not cultivate, and which the district accepts without due consideration. Sometimes the ground is selected in a ravine, or perhaps on a hill, or some other place difficult of access, forcing the children to walk across fields instead of along the traveled roads in order to reach it.

The school-house should be properly constructed in the arrangement of the halls, rooms, and stairways; of the heating, ventilation, lighting, and seating. Some school-rooms are not in good shape for auditory purposes. Every school-house should be so well heated that it is comfortable in every part; it should be commodious, so that every person in it shall have enough breathing and working space; it should be well lighted, so that the constant use of the eyes need not result in injury to these most useful and sensitive of organs; it should be well ventilated, so that the workers within it shall be supplied with pure air, and yet not in such a manner as to expose any one to the death-dealing draughts; it should be supplied with comfortable seats and desks adapted to the sizes of the pupils who occupy them; and it should be well supplied with such other things as facilitate the work of instruction. There should be a clock in every room. Time is an important element in the management of a school. Work must be begun on time, continued full time, finished on time. The habit of being on time in the performance of every duty should be formed early in the life of every child, and a clock ever before him, telling the time, is needed among the first items of furniture in a school-room. A teacher who fails to be on time can not succeed any more than can a business man who is always behind time. The railroad train never waits for the laggard.

How was a school ever successful without a blackboard? is a question that we ask nowadays. I can recollect a place in Illinois where a heated discussion arose in regard to the introduction of a blackboard into a church. This was at an early day, and nobody in that part of the country had ever seen a blackboard. A man came out from the State of New York and taught arithmetic and a little English grammar, and he wanted a blackboard. He was conducting his school in a Baptist church, and the elders opposed the use of anything black, as they thought it might be begotten of the devil, and have a bad influence on their spiritual welfare. But he finally persuaded them to allow it, and when Sunday came there was the blackboard, not larger than our penmanship charts, and they turned the black part to the wall in one corner of the church. Ideas, new ideas, spread with wonderful rapidity, and now a school-house without a blackboard would seem like a wagon without wheels. A blackboard ought to extend entirely around the four sides of the room. It must be made low, so that the little children can use it, and high enough for the larger children. And there are maps and charts—the tools without which a teacher can not do all the work of the school properly.

The water furnished for school children should be pure and fresh; and, if taken from a well or cistern, should be drawn and exposed to the air in pails. No well or cistern should be covered to exclude the air, for air helps to keep the water pure and healthful. Recent experiments show that more people die of typhoid fever caused by drinking impure water than from any other one cause. Not long since one of the ablest mathematicians in this country died at the early age of thirty-seven, and his death was attributed to drinking impure cistern-water. School children must be supplied with pure water to drink. We have no right to be careless about this. There must be no poison in their drink, in the food they eat, nor in the air they breathe.

Play-Grounds.

A play-ground is almost as necessary to a school-house as the latter is to a district. It should be large, well fenced in, and there should be trees and flowers and pleasant walks to add to its attractions. The love of the beautiful ought always to be cherished in the hearts of the children, for this love has a strong and permanent influence in molding character, and in preparing them for useful, happy lives. And, when the walks and grounds are made beautiful, the children should be encouraged to use them, to care for them. And, too, the decoration of the school-rooms themselves by the children should be encouraged. Let them bring flowers and pictures, if they will; and, be the offering ever so simple, express yourself pleased, thus giving great joy to the heart of the little child.

Myopia.

Before taking up the second division of our subject we will refer again to the proper lighting of school-rooms, in order to call attention to the care of the eyes. In this country and in Europe much complaint has been made of the *myopia*, or near-sightedness, of so many pupils in the schools. More than sixty per cent of the students who go through the German schools leave there near-sighted. There must be a reason for this, and many physicians who have investigated the subject agree in thinking that much of it might be avoided by an observance of the following points: The light should not be allowed to come directly in the face of the child, but from the left side. Care should be exercised in regard to the amount of light. If there is not enough light in a room, there results an unnatural and injurious expansion of the pupil of the eye if an effort is made to use the eyes.

Again, teachers should see to it that children do not sit with their bodies bent forward and downward, nor with the eyes too close to their books, nor hold their books so that the rays of light strike their books at too obtuse angles.

Teachers have better opportunities for preventing or discovering optical defects in pupils than parents, and should at once notify the latter when there are indications of an abnormal or of a diseased condition of the eyes.

Classification and Promotion.

The most difficult problem, especially for young teachers going into country schools, is that of the organization of classes. The statements of the children can not be relied upon to give full data for classification, nor can reports left by a former teacher always be trusted, as they give so little information on this subject. Frequently boys go to school one winter, and get nearly through the arithmetic, say from fractions to square-root, during a three months' term of school. The next year comes a new teacher. Some of these boys do not return, and some new ones come in. Those who return usually have to begin just where they did the year before, and pursue the same old track. This goes on sometimes for six or seven years, and the pupils never get any farther in their studies than they did in the first winter.

Every teacher who is employed in a country school should leave a record in which are the names of all the pupils, with a distinct statement of the advancement of each, so that a new teacher need have no difficulty in organizing the school without loss of time.

There should be a definite basis of classification, and

this the teacher should know and follow. If one teacher grades on spelling, and his successor on penmanship, and a third on something else—each on his own hobby—no good results can be secured in a school.

It is generally conceded by educators that all classification in schools should be based upon reading and arithmetic, the former in the lower grades, and the latter in all the more advanced classes.

If there be a large pupil, whose mental powers seem tolerably well developed, and he can apply himself more closely than others, he should be placed in more advanced classes, even though he can not read very well. By this means he will be able to derive all the benefit possible in the short time he remains in school.

Some time since I prepared the following Course of Study and Daily Programme for country schools, making it extend over a period of eight school years, allowing six months to the year. Many pupils will complete it in less time. The school is arranged in two departments, *primary* and *grammar*, four years' time given to each department, and each year being divided into two terms of three months each. The year and grade are made to correspond. The fractions indicate what part of a subject is completed during a term. The star indicates that the instruction is entirely oral, and that the pupil does not have a text-book. In language and primary geography the oral instruction is supplemented by the book. The object of this course of study is to systematize the work in country schools, to aid teachers in the work of classification, and to secure better results than can be done under the loose plan, with nothing definite in view.

SCHOOL MANAGEMENT. 27

COURSE OF STUDY FOR COUNTRY SCHOOLS.

STUDIES AND TEXT-BOOKS. * Oral.	Primary Department.								Grammar Department.							
	First Year. I Grade.		Second Year. II Grade.		Third Year. III Grade.		Fourth Year. IV Grade.		Fifth Year. V Grade.		Sixth Year. VI Grade.		Seventh Year. VII Grade.		Eighth Year. VIII Grade.	
	First Term.	Second Term.	First Term.	Second Term.	First Term.	Second Term.	First Term.	Second Term.	First Term.	Second Term.	First Term.	Second Term.	First Term.	Second Term.	First Term.	Second Term.
First Reader	1/2	1/2														
Second Reader			1/2	1/2												
Third Reader					1/2	1/2										
Oral and Element. Arithmetic	*	*	*	*	1/4	1/4	1/4	1/4								
Language and Composition	*	*	*	*	1/4*	1/4*	1/4*	1/4*								
First Geography	*	*	*	*	1/4*	1/4*	1/4*	1/4*								
Writing—Drawing	1/2 First Princpl's	1/2 pies	1/4	1/4	1/4	1/4	1/4	1/4	1/2							
Fourth Reader									1/2	1/2	1/2					
Fifth Reader											1/2	1/2	1/2	1/2	1/2	1/2
Spelling and Etymology											1/2	1/2	1/2	1/2	1/2	1/2
Practical Arithmetic									1/2	1/2	1/4	1/4	1/4	1/4	1/4	1/4
Intellectual Arithmetic										1/2	1/2	1/4	1/4	1/4	1/4	
Grammar and Composition											1/4	1/4	1/4	1/4	1/4	1/4
Geography											1/4	1/4	1/4	1/4		
U. S. History and Civil Gov't													1/4	1/4	1/4	1/4
Physiology															1/2	1/2

Many persons have an idea that the graded-school system is a kind of Procrustean bed upon which pupils are fitted without regard to their interests.

The mechanically graded school and the heterogeneous country school represent the two extremes of the common-school system. In one it is all system reduced to a monotonous routine, while the other presents all the varied beauties arising from the advantages (?) of frequent promotions—a systemless school.

There is certainly need of reform in some graded schools, in which the whole machinery has become petrified, and a little shaking up would do the rigid fossil some good. But, while this is true, it is also true that the introduction of some system of classification into the ungraded and country schools is not only necessary but most desirable.

In classifying pupils, there are some questions which are applicable to all schools. For this reason their introduction just here seems not inappropriate, and may be a help to teachers in either city or country schools:

1. Has the pupil ever attended school?
2. What does he actually know?
3. After he has entered school, if at any time he is able to do the work of a more advanced class, is it the part of wisdom to promote him?
4. What influence on his health would an undue stimulus have?
5. Is he old enough to be rushed through his studies, and has he the constitution to bear it?
6. What are the home influences?
7. If he has been in school, why did he fall behind his class?

The last question arises more frequently in graded than in ungraded schools.

In the graded schools are representatives of the following classes of pupils:

(*a*) Those entering school for the first time.

(*b*) Those who have finished the work of their grade.

(*c*) Those who are able to go more rapidly than the average class, and are therefore the subjects of special promotion.

(*d*) Those who have fallen behind in the regular class-work and can not keep up.

Only in rare instances, if a pupil is regular in attendance, does he fail to "pass."

The work laid out for each term is what the child of average ability is capable of doing. Many can do more.

One of the chief reasons why the charge is made that children make slow progress in the graded schools is that those making the assertion fail to distinguish between what young men and young women can do in school in two or three years, and the inability of little children to do the same amount of work in the same time.

Maturity of mind is required to make extraordinary progress, and small children, unless precocious, do not have it.

Were the pupils kept out of school till twelve or fifteen years of age, they could then do the work of the graded-school course of study in two or three years; but we must consider this subject as it at present exists.

Suppose the utmost tension is given to the graded-school system, are there not then weighty objections which play an important part in the education of children?

(*a*) The frequent change of teachers is one of the disadvantages of the country schools. Now, if it be injurious to change teachers every few months in country schools, how can the reverse of this be true for town and city schools? I know of no rules in reasoning that will warrant contradictory conclusions from the same premises, and both conclusions be correct.

(*b*) It does not answer to say that the pupils are hurried through the lower schools till they get into the high school, and will then remain under the influence of the same teachers for three or four years.

(*c*) Introducing an unnatural excitant has a tendency to destroy the main object for which public schools are supported and patronized. The idea, whether intentional or not, is held out to both teachers and pupils to prepare for promotion by "stuffing," "cramming," or "packing." These are the feeble words used to express the hurry and waste and haste in order to get through and make a show. Teachers feel that, if their brightest pupils are not hurried onward at race-horse speed, their services are not duly appreciated, and there is danger of losing their positions. This is certainly a serious objection which I have not seen satisfactorily answered. Under high pressure, the object of education is not the acquisition of knowledge for its own sake, but the delusive phantom of promotion, which is always tantalizing to the mind of the sensitive pupil. The pupil, when leaving school, should go away with the conviction that he has finished the school-work up to date.

(*d*) The health of the pupil in this race is neglected,

and the intense strain on the nervous system destroys the natural and healthy action of the vital functions, thus insidiously undermining the constitution and laying the foundation for disease.

By exercising reasonable care in classifying at the beginning of the school-term, few mistakes will be made, and these may in a short time be corrected. The remedy is in the hands of the principal and teacher. Pupils should be promoted because they have completed the preceding work, or have the ability to go on with a higher class. Promotions for other reasons are usually a positive injury to all parties concerned.

In the graded schools we call the first year in school the first grade, the second year the second grade, and so on through the eighth grade, after which comes the work of the high school. A difficult problem now presents itself for solution, and that is the number of classes and the number of studies to be taken up by the pupils.

Possibly three new branches of study besides reading are as many as any pupil can pursue profitably at one time. Writing, drawing, and music are properly classed as "drills," but drawing is an excellent exercise for training the hand, the eye, the judgment, and the imagination.

If a student has Greek, Latin, and mathematics, he has enough new work. These are the studies usually pursued in high-school and college classes. Some pupils take more, but the effect upon the health is usually bad. Hundreds of college students are wrecking their whole lives because teachers encourage them in this course. Year after year I look into the faces of pupils whose vital energies are being exhausted by mental overwork.

Movements of Classes.

Suppose a young lady goes for the first time into a school-room to fill a vacancy occasioned by the absence of the regular teacher. The children are full of life. It is time for recitation. How shall she call out a class? One bright little girl reports that her teacher says "Attention!" and then taps with her pencil. The first tap means "turn," the second "rise," the third "pass," and the children pass to their places on the "line." This is a good way to give signals, and the movements are just what are needed. But suppose the teacher has been a little unsystematic. The new teacher says, "The class in the first reader will take their places." They run to their places, each child trying to be first. There is confusion, and it is difficult to get them into line, and to watch them. But, if the teacher is quiet and dignified, she will succeed, even though she does not understand the work of the regular teacher. It is a good plan for her to explain in this way: "When I say 'one,' turn your feet into the aisle; when I say 'two,' rise; and when I say 'three,' pass to the place where you recite your lessons."

I have seen children going to their places with their hands behind them, and walking on their toes. Old men sometimes walk with their hands behind them, but is it natural for children? Teach children to walk and to stand flat-footed. Do not distort the natural form of a child for the sake of a death-like stillness in the school-room.

In returning them to their seats at the close of a recitation, the same plan should be pursued, first calling "Attention!" which means to close open books and take position ready to obey the signals which will be given for them to turn and to pass to seats. The plan adopted by many teachers of having them stand at their seats till all are in place, and then be seated at one signal, is a good one.

Movements at the Blackboard.

Each member of the class should have his place assigned him. Then, suppose the lesson is in arithmetic, and there are five problems, let the class number in sections of "five," each member of a section to have the problem corresponding to his number. Then, at a signal, all turn in one direction—to the left—till they face the board. If the names of pupils are not already written, at a signal they write names and numbers. The next signal means "work." After a reasonable time has been given for placing solutions on the board, "Attention!" should be called, when all should turn *from* the board, this time turning to the right. Explanations are then called for and given. At the close of the recitation, the signal "erase" being given, they obey it; then, at the closing signal, "attention!" they turn from the board and stand in position ready to obey the signals which seat them.

Programme.

In a well-managed school there is a definite time for the beginning and close of every exercise. There must be a time-table so arranged and placed that the teacher may know just what each pupil is doing at any hour—

that is, what lessons are being prepared and by what classes, as well as what recitations are being conducted. It is quite as necessary to assign time for preparation of lessons as for recitation and recreation. In making out a programme, it should be so arranged that the different classes have an equal number of recitations. Again, that programme is the best which provides that no two successive recitations are on the same subject, because those who are studying are less apt to have their attention diverted from their own lessons, or to get assistance of a character which relieves them of the exertion required to master their own difficulties. It is also important that the programme be placed so that all in the room can see it. The pupils should be taught to understand it, and thus learn to be systematic in their work.

As a fitting conclusion to this subject of programmes, I place here for inspection one which I prepared for country schools. It shows when each class recites, and what; and, at the same time, what lessons are being prepared by the other classes. The recitations are printed in italics.

The same general plan is that best adapted to graded schools, the teacher making necessary changes in the details.

PROGRAMME FOR COUNTRY SCHOOLS.

TIME TABLE.	VIII and VII Years. Class A.	VI and V Years. Class B.	IV and III Years. Class C.	II and I Year. Class D.
8.50 to 9.00 10	Opening Exercises.			
9.00 to 9.25 25	Grammar.	Grammar.	Read and spell.	Read and spell.
9.25 to 9.35 10	Arithmetic.	Grammar.	Read and spell.	*Read and spell.*
9.35 to 9.55 20	Arithmetic.	*Grammar.*	Read and spell.	Write numbers on slate.
9.55 to 10.10 15	*Arithmetic.*	Arithmetic.	*Read and spell.*	Write numbers on slate.
10.10 to 10.30 20	*Writing or drawing.*	*Writing or drawing.*	*Writing or drawing.*	*Writing or drawing.*
10.30 to 10.40 10	Recess.	Recess.	Recess.	Recess.
10.40 to 11.05 25	*Arithmetic.*	Arithmetic.	Arithmetic.	Read and spell.
11.05 to 11.15 10	History, U. S.	Arithmetic.	Arithmetic.	*Read and spell.*
11.15 to 11.35 20	History, U. S.	*Arithmetic.*	*Arithmetic.*	Write reading-lesson on slate.
11.35 to 11.50 15	History, U. S.	History, U. S.	*Arithmetic.*	Write reading-lesson on slate.
11.50 to 12.00 10	History, U. S.	History, U. S.	Geography.	*Write numbers on blackboard.*
12.00 to 1.00 60	Noon.	Noon.	Noon.	Noon.
1.00 to 1.25 25	*History, U. S.*	*History, U. S.*	Geography.	Read and spell.
1.25 to 1.35 10	Physiology.	Geography.	Geography.	*Read and spell.*
1.35 to 1.50 15	Physiology.	Geography.	*Geography.*	Writing language exercise.
1.50 to 2.10 20	Physiology.	*Geography.*	Read and spell.	Writing language exercise.
2.10 to 2.30 20	*Physiology.*	Reading or etymology.	Read and spell.	Writing language exercise.
2.30 to 2.40 10	Recess.	Recess.	Recess.	Recess.
2.40 to 2.50 10	Reading or etymology.	Reading or etymology.	Read and spell.	Writing language exercise.
2.50 to 3.10 20	*Reading or etymology.*	*Reading or etymology.*	Read and spell.	
3.10 to 3.25 15	Intellectual arithmetic.	Intellectual arithmetic.	*Read and spell.*	
3.25 to 3.45 20	*Intellectual arithmetic.*	*Intellectual arithmetic.*	Language exercise.	
3.45 to 3.55 10	Grammar.	Grammar.	*Language exercise.*	Dismiss.
3.55 to 4.00 05	Dismiss.	Dismiss.	Dismiss.	

EXPLANATIONS.—This programme shows when each class recites, and, at the same time, what lessons the other classes are preparing. The recitation is printed in *italics.*

Analysis.—School Management.

I. School-House.
  a. Location.
  b. Construction.
    1. Heating.
    2. Ventilating.
    3. Lighting.
    4. Seating.
  c. Well and out-buildings.
  d. Furniture.
    1. Clock.
    2. Blackboard.
    3. Maps.
    4. Charts, etc.
  e. Play-grounds.
    1. Walks.
    2. Trees.
    3. Flowers.

II. Organization of Classes.
  a. Basis.
  b. Ungraded schools.
  c. Graded schools.
  d. High schools.
  e. Colleges.

III. Movements of Classes.
  a. How called.
  b. How seated.
  c. At blackboard.
  d. How dismissed.

IV. Programme.
  a. Time-table.
  b. Preparation.
  c. Recitation.
  d. Subjects.
    1. Order.
    2. Alternation.

CHAPTER III.

PRINCIPLES OF CLASS MANAGEMENT.

Classes having been organized, how to manage them becomes an important problem for the teacher to solve. Very few teachers would hesitate to confirm the statement that "attention must be secured before instruction can be given, or any school work successfully done." How to secure attention is the first lesson for the teacher to learn. The ability to do this when appearing before a class of restless boys and girls is an all-important qualification for a teacher to possess, and especially so if the class is composed of small children.

It is not easy to tell in words just how to get the attention of a class. Some persons seem gifted with the power to secure and hold the attention of any with whom they enter into conversation. Some call this power magnetism; we can not tell certainly. It may consist in the skill with which they can present a subject; it may be in the tones of the voice. Some teachers with soft, low tones have secured what commands could not have done. It was not the authority of the teacher over the attention of the child—that the teacher can not command in words. The faculty of attention in the child must be cultivated, so that it shall come under the control of his own will, which, in its turn, must be guided by the teacher's will.

Suppose a teacher appears before his class and tries to explain something about a lesson. Half the class is inattentive. The teacher is conscious of the fact, and yet he does not know what to do. The pupils discover his helplessness and take advantage of it. The teacher fails, and the school is demoralized.

Various devices are resorted to by teachers who can not easily secure the attention of children. They tell anecdotes; they offer rewards; they threaten to punish, and do many other things equally futile. It may be that the real secret of securing attention consists in knowing how to adapt the instruction to the capacity of the learners, how to interest them, and get them to tell what they know. As stated before, attention is not secured by commanding it, but by arousing the mind of the child to an interest in the subject. Hence, an important part of the teacher's work is so to train the child that he can, by the exercise of his own will, concentrate his attention upon whatever subject he has to consider. Children do not, at first, know how to do this; it is a lesson they must learn.

When a person has learned how to fix his mind upon one subject to the exclusion of all else, despite outside influences, he becomes the thinker, the learned man, the great man; and this power is what distinguishes him from the ignorant man. It is not absent-mindedness, it is not forgetfulness, but it is the ability to take a subject, think only of it, turn it over and over, as it were, in the mind till it is understood; beginning in the darkness of ignorance, soon letting in a little gleam of light, the very faintest ray, perhaps, but leading out into the broad sunlight of knowledge through what seemed impenetrable darkness, the darkness of ignorance.

The teacher who would lead a class out of ignorance into knowledge, and attain the highest success in class-management, must himself possess this power—that is, he must be able to bring his own faculty of attention entirely under the control of his own will. Then, and then only, is he prepared to control the attention of a class.

We can conceive how a stone can grow by accretions to the outside, but we can not conceive how a human being can grow physically by such a process. It is true he might be encased in the shell of a mollusk, and thus appear to be enlarged externally, but it would not be true growth. Neither would it be true growth for the child to be covered all over, if that were possible, with knowledge as with a plaster.

Physical growth is produced by the assimilation of the material used for food and drink, and conveyed to the different parts of the body. We do not quite understand the process, but the material is gathered and passes through the changes wrought by the various organs of digestion till it is prepared for assimilation and enters into the life-blood of the individual.

And thus we grow intellectually. Information—food for thought—is gathered through the senses into the mind, and by the mind itself is prepared for assimilation, giving mental growth in the very effort.

Again, the teacher should not forget that his pupils must get knowledge, must have ideas, and must learn how to express these ideas. If the teacher does all the talking, all the reciting, the pupils are being robbed of the benefits to be derived from the recitation. The pupil must recite, not the teacher. Can a child learn to walk if not permitted to use his own feet? Can he learn how to express his thoughts if not permitted to try? The teacher must guide, must lead over the difficult places, must encourage the feeble, but must not do the work, must not recite for the child.

A hungry child remains hungry still if he has but looked wistfully on while another has eaten the food. The hungry one represents the pupil who desires knowledge, and the other the teacher who recites, who talks all the time. What would be thought of the teacher who should argue as follows: "Should I not recite at least half the time? Am I not here for that purpose? Am I not to help the pupils? I am the teacher, and I must talk about the lesson to them. I can do it better than they can."

Neither should the teacher be an interrogation-point, doing nothing but asking questions, or reading them at the bottom of the page while the pupils follow with their fingers and glance at the answers as given above. That teacher is wise who is able to control his tongue and not talk too much. The apostle was right when he called the tongue an "unruly member."

The teacher must explain lessons, but the explanations should be appropriate and pointed, so that even the dullest pupils can understand them.

The above point suggests another. The teacher should manage to reach every pupil during every recitation, but no one should know when he is to be called on. The question should be asked first, and in such a manner that it will apply to one pupil as well as to another, making all feel responsible for the answer, and then some one called on to recite. It is not as though each had a separate "grist to grind," and must stand in the line waiting his turn, as did the people in olden times, when each of those who went to the mill had to wait in the line "till his corn was ground and he could get his meal."

Knowledge is not like meal; each can take all, and yet all is left for the next hungry mind. No one is robbed, and all gain mental strength as well as knowledge. The faculty of attention is receiving cultivation, and the teacher is no longer troubled about how to secure attention. The difficult problem is being solved in a safer way than the "going up and down" method formerly so much in vogue, and the lesson of the day is not lost.

In certain schools it was the custom for the pupil who came first to school to recite first; and, if there was a class recitation, the head pupil recited first, and then waited till every other member of the class had been called on, when it came his turn again. If it was a reading lesson, the head boy read his "verse," whether in prose or poetry; the second boy his, and so on down the class. If there were not enough "verses to go round," the recitation was ended. Occasionally, the words in the reading lesson were spelled. In the spelling classes, a good speller would spell nearly all the words. If a pupil missed a word, it was passed quickly to the "next," and the "next," and the "next," till it got to a good speller, who usually stood at the head and did most of the spelling.

How will that compare with a recitation like this? It was a class in Latin, and all the boys and all the girls wanted to answer. If one happened to make a mistake, the hands of all the others went up, showing that all were held responsible for the lesson. The teacher called on one after another, but in such a manner that no one knew when his turn would come. In a certain celebrated college in which there are many very learned men, I once heard a lesson in chemistry recited. The class was seated, and the "professor" called on Mr. A to recite, and Mr. A stood up and told all he knew about the subject, and was excused. Then the "professor" called on Mr. B, and Mr. B gave attention. But, while Mr. A was reciting, I noticed that Mr. Y and Mr. Z were busy upon other work, and did not seem at all interested in what Mr. A was saying. When Mr. B got through, Mr. C prepared for consultation, and waited with a great show of respect for the question which he knew was sure to come, and his recitation was a repetition of what Mr. A and Mr. B had said. In this way the very distinguished professor worked on till he got through with Mr. Z. This, I learned, was considered a model recitation. I should add that the very celebrated professor would not allow students to perform experiments in chemistry "lest they break some of the little jars."

The same system, I am sorry to say, is pursued in some other institutions of learning. There is this difficulty—so many teachers can only *copy*, copy, COPY, doing just what their grandfathers did, and in precisely the same way. Some teachers still insist upon doing everything just as it was done by those who came over in the early days from England and Holland. In these later days we oppose some of those old methods, and say they are not the best. Not a few living persons can remember when geometry was taught by " rote." The "professor" was often a person who knew nothing about geometry. A certain number of propositions were given for a lesson, and their numbers were written on pieces of paper and placed on the table. The members of the class, one after the other, drew each his lot, and examined it to see whether it contained a prize or blank. Whoever drew a numbered paper recited *verbatim* the demonstration of the proposition having the same number; but those who drew blanks had nothing to do.

The temptation to encourage bright pupils to do all the reciting is one which teachers should resist. The bright children might be benefited, but such a course is intellectual death to the dull ones. The latter should receive increased attention; the points over which they struggle should be developed, and the whole class benefited thereby.

Let us take this circle, O, to represent the positive knowledge that is possessed by the pupil. Beyond this he has some vague ideas of some subjects, and these may be supposed to form a hazy outline to the circle of his definite knowledge. This circle is to be enlarged by investigations in the misty regions beyond.

Different subjects lie in different directions. In one direction there may be natural history, and the teacher desires to expand the pupil's mind in that direction.

To do this, some definite questions must be asked; the pupil set to thinking. He must be encouraged to tell what he thinks, and then be required to get some definite knowledge by further investigation out in that misty region. He has been shown how to find his way, and it is now time to observe a principle, too often overlooked, that the teacher should get a pupil to do all he can for himself, and not do his work for him. "Why," says a student, "is it not better for me, if I have studied a subject over and found it difficult, to get the teacher to do it for me? It would save me so much labor, and it is the teacher's business to help me, to make my work easy for me." Pupils would usually be pleased to have the teacher do all the difficult work for them; but those who can be induced to study a subject and master its difficulties alone will be most profited. The teacher should suggest the direction and method of study for pupils, and then, having put them on the road to certain knowledge, watch their progress. Having given them the clew, he should be sure that they have made an effort before he helps, and then not help them too much; only just enough to help them help themselves. By their own mental effort comes their own mental growth. We are told that one of the Greeks had a problem to solve, and that, after he had spent some time in studying it over, he noticed that when he got into a bath-tub partly filled with water the water rose, and that when he got out it sank again. He thought of this for some time, and then rushed out crying "Eureka!" He had solved his difficult problem; he could find the cubical contents of an irregular solid by immersing it in a vessel full of water and measuring the water that ran over.

A teacher asked a class to tell him the number of cubic inches in a large irregular stone. They looked at it, but there was no solid like it. Some tried to divide it into triangular pyramids. They examined it very carefully. The teacher gave them more time for the study of the problem. The next day came, and several members of the class had learned that they could measure it by putting the stone into water and seeing how far the water rose in the vessel. They remembered their own discovery better than if the teacher had told them, and the gain in mental power was of more value to them than any help the teacher might have given. Men have been known to work on one problem five years or more before they conquered its difficulties.

Assistance must, of course, be given; but when and how given are important questions. A certain teacher whom I once knew used to walk around the school-room to see how her pupils were getting along. If they were at work on a "sum," she would explain it and "work it out" for them. If they were studying a geography lesson, she would pronounce and explain all the *hard* words. She would even remain after school to help them prepare their lessons. She made a mistake in doing this. Help should be given before the whole class and during the time of recitation, and never at any other time. Pupils may complain of this, but it is the better way, especially for advanced pupils. Why? may be asked. Because, if an explanation is necessary, the whole class should hear it given; the teacher of large classes can not afford to give private tuition to each member. With such a precedent established in the case of one pupil, others will soon demand it, and the teacher dare not then refuse, and soon becomes a slave to her pupils, who will neglect purposely the preparation of lessons at the proper time. Inattention results during the recitation, and the pupils are forming the bad habit of "procrastination." Remember that part of the time of a recitation rightfully belongs to explanations for which the pupils then may ask. And it is just as important that they should improve this time as any other, and be held to strict account for it. I have seen schools in which the teacher, while engaged in conducting a recitation, was continually interrupted by pupils coming from their seats to ask unimportant questions, and to get help which they did not need. If they are permitted to do this, is it possible for the recitation to be of any value to the class? Can a teacher do more than one thing at a time?

Just imagine a case like this: The teacher is conducting a recitation in arithmetic. A boy who belongs to another class is preparing a spelling-lesson; he looks at the first word, names the letters over to himself, runs up to the teacher, who stops whatever she is doing to pronounce the word for him. By the time he gets to his seat he has named over the letters in another word. He drops into his seat, but bounces out immediately, and runs to the teacher, who stops again to pronounce the second word for him. The performance is repeated again and again, till the teacher has pronounced every word in his lesson. He is not the only one. Other pupils have as much right to demand help as he has, and the continual interruption becomes an intolerable nuisance.

A strict observance of the rule "to help only during the time of recitation" will not interfere with a general supervision of all pupils in a room. If they are under good discipline, and have been properly trained at the beginning of the term, they will not think of interrupting a recitation, but will devote the time to quiet study.

Formerly, very little attention was given in schools to any written work outside of the regular lessons in writing. It is now quite the custom to divide the time of recitation about equally between oral and written work, and, while the benefits to be derived from oral recitation are not lost, the written work affords better opportunity for the teacher to reach and criticise the work of every one.

It has been said before, but will bear repeating, "Train pupils to use their own language." Let each express his ideas in his own way, then criticise and correct. Be not too severe and discourage him, but make criticisms so as not to wound his feelings. You can test the accuracy of knowledge by the language used, unless it is a verbatim reproduction of that found in the book.

There must be system, vigor, life in all good school-work. The teaching should be adapted to the capacity of the pupil, and the steps in passing from the known should be made easy.

What a teacher says should be said in a definite, incisive manner, showing confidence in self and inspiring it in pupils. The teacher must be wide awake, must believe in his own ability to succeed, but must keep in mind the fact that he ought to be progressive, and never think himself too old to learn. He may be self-confident, but not egotistical; must have that kind of self-confidence which insures success.

II. **Class Management.**
    1. Secure attention by right methods.
    2. Adapt instruction to capacities.

III. **The Recitation.**
    1. Length.
        a. Primary classes.
        b. Grammar classes.
        c. High schools.
        d. Normal schools.
        e. Colleges.
    2. Division of time.
        a. Review.   1. Definition.
        b. Lesson of the day.   2. Object.
        c. Criticisms.   3. How?
        d. General information. 4. When?
        e. Talk about the next lesson. 5. By whom?
    3. Assignment of lesson.
        a. Subjects rather than pages.
        b. Lessons too short rather than too long.
        c. Instruction—how to prepare.
    4. Object.
        a. To gain knowledge.
        b. Mental development.

CHAPTER IV.

METHODS OF CONDUCTING RECITATIONS—DIRECTIONS TO PUPILS—DIRECTIONS TO TEACHERS.

THERE are three elements to be considered in connection with every recitation, not including the subject-matter: First, the method of conducting the recitation; secondly, the pupils or persons to be benefited by the recitation; and, thirdly, the teacher or person who conducts the recitation.

Under methods there are three divisions: recitations may be entirely oral, entirely written, or a combination of the two methods. In advanced classes it is well to have recitations about half oral and half written.

There are advantages in both oral and written recitations, but neither should be used to the exclusion of the other.

If a recitation be oral, it must be either individual or concert, or both, the time occupied in recitation being divided between the two.

If the recitations are by individuals, the choice lies between the consecutive and promiscuous methods. By the consecutive method, the pupil at the head of the class is required to answer first, then the next, and so on, in the order of their positions in the class. A serious objection to this method is that pupils soon learn to keep tally with the number of questions, and make close calculations as to what questions are likely to come to them, and will learn to answer only those, neglecting other parts of the lesson entirely. The plan of calling on pupils promiscuously is much better, securing more surely the attention of the whole class to every part of the lesson, and making each member of the class feel that he is responsible for the answer to every question that may be asked, or for the omission of any point in the lesson if the recitation is by other than the method of questions and answers.

As a general thing, recitations in concert should be avoided, and, if used at all, should be very sparingly used, never exclusively. Yet the concert recitation has, perhaps, advantages. Some children are very timid, and it is difficult to get them to speak so as to be heard. A concert recitation may give courage to such as these, but, if the courage thus gained is not sustained and applied to individual work, even this is a doubtful advantage, and courage had better be developed in some other way. A very skillful teacher may use it in teaching reading when pupils have difficulty in pronouncing words, or are inclined to read too rapidly, or when he wishes to harmonize voices and bring them to a uniform pitch. It is also useful in teaching inflections. Few teachers, however, are able to conduct concert recitations without allowing pupils to acquire the sing-song habit, which, once acquired, is almost impossible to get rid of.

When a teacher can not prevent this sing-song in concert recitation, he should banish the method from his school-room. The effort to counteract the sing-song habit produces results but little better in reading. Here is an illustration: Not long since I heard a class of intelligent children read. In conversation, their words were very naturally spoken; but when they read it was very different. They had often recited in concert, and could sing it off in fine style. To break up this habit, they were required to stop after every syllable. This, too, was a severe struggle. Every feature of their faces assumed a rigid aspect. The muscles of their bodies were strained to the highest pitch, and they read this simple exercise, "Gyp was going to the mill, and he saw a frog," with a laborious effort, cutting and snapping at the words in a frightful manner. There was no variation in pitch, there was no attention to emphasis, and every syllable was jerked out and snapped off as if the pupils were afraid of their own voices, which sounded so unnatural because of the great exertion they were making to read as the teacher had directed. A small boy was asked to read it. It was a repetition of what the class had done. When he closed the book and repeated it, he threw off that stiffness which hampered him when he tried to read from the book, and his tones at once dropped into the conversational style. When this habit is once acquired, it takes months to break it up.

It is best, I think, to conduct the recitations of small children by asking questions which they must answer. They have not the power of continued attention, and should not be required to do more than they can do easily till they have learned how to study, and they can not study so as to master a topic till they have learned how to read that from which they must study for recitation.

Timid children must have a little help and much encouragement until they get well acquainted.

For larger children, the topical method is used to great advantage, as it makes them rely more upon themselves to remember all the points in the lesson, and forces them to greater effort in the use of language. The questions asked by the teacher are often very suggestive, giving a clew to the pupil which helps him, even though they may not be leading questions.

If the classes are very large, a variation of the topical method is sometimes adopted. The different topics are assigned to different pupils, each being required to report upon his topic such information as he can get. This gives a collection of reports upon which they can institute comparisons, study and discuss relations, and so develop the thinking faculties. This method is particularly adapted to classes in rhetoric, literature, and the natural sciences.

Teaching by lectures can scarcely be called a recitation, but the same results are sought to be accomplished. In the German universities the students never recite. They listen to the lectures, take notes, and study up the subject. Then, as I understand it, when they are to be examined for graduation, each one goes alone before the faculty, and is questioned by all its members.

Sometimes it is advantageous for a recitation to take the form of a discussion. Among older students, this is both interesting and profitable, and is admirably adapted to some of the subjects taught in normal schools and colleges.

METHODS OF CONDUCTING RECITATIONS. 53

Again, there is the reciprocal method, which may be profitably used in ordinary school-work, and in most of the grades. In this, the teacher asks a question, and calls on "A" to recite. When "A" has recited, he asks another question, and calls on "Z" to recite. "Z" answers, and calls on some one else to recite. In this way the whole lesson is recited, the questions and answers passing from one to another till all have taken part. If one pupil can not give a complete answer, he may call on some one else to finish what he has begun. This method is particularly useful, in that it is apt to excite considerable animation among the members of a class.

Recitations entirely written are not common, nor are they to be desired except for examinations.

The combination of oral and written recitations is usually that in which pupils are required to write a *diagram* or outline of the subject of the lesson, and then to recite from what they have written. It can not be very well employed with small children, but with larger ones, and through the school course, beginning in the middle grades, it is valuable, because it formulates and systematizes the knowledge gained, so arranging it in the mind as to make it available whenever it is needed for use.

Knowledge to be available must be classified. He who does this by means of outlines, or diagrams, has his information at his command and ready for use, and is far better prepared than he who leaves it "lying around loose."

DIRECTIONS TO PUPILS.

There are directions to be given to pupils which they must be required to observe. The first is this: "Stand or sit erect." Some of them have shoulders that tip forward; some have not a strong digestive apparatus, and, if they are allowed to bend forward, their vital organs will be cramped and weakened. This direction has special reference to the care of their health, and upon its observance much of their success as students depends. It does not mean that they should always sit bolt upright, though it is better to do this than to acquire the habit of dropping the shoulders forward and contracting the chest, so that the lungs can not expand as they need to do in performing their functions.

A close observer will notice that a person breathing takes every fourth or fifth breath fuller, deeper than the others, and thus unconsciously performs the act of expelling impure air from the lungs. The person whose blood is in good condition is in good health; but this is impossible if the blood is not purified by contact with pure air as it passes through the lungs on its way back to the heart after its journey as scavenger through the circulatory system. Drowsiness is a result of impure blood, and perfect mental development is checked.

The class must understand all signals, and move promptly and quietly when they are given. It is worth while to spend several hours drilling pupils to a military precision in all school movements. The teacher who will do this establishes his authority in the school at the beginning, saves time, and avoids much subsequent friction which might otherwise occur.

Not only must pupils be taught to move promptly, but quietly; there should be no stamping, no tramping. This has been spoken of before; but repetitions are sometimes necessary—they do not need to walk with their hands behind them, nor on their toes. They can walk quietly, easily, and naturally, placing their feet firmly and squarely on the floor. The tip-toe walking required by many teachers in order to avoid noise is unnatural and ungraceful, resulting too often in permanent awkwardness, and should not be tolerated a moment. Suppose they do make a little noise; better that than to destroy the natural grace of childish movements.

Pupils should at all times be polite to their teacher and to one another. A strict observance of this rule will make school-life both pleasant and profitable, and form a habit which will be an advantage to them when they come in contact with the world in after life.

Each pupil must recite in his own words. This is a necessary requirement. It does not mean that his language must be elegant; it may be even incorrect; but his ability to express whatever ideas he may have in his own words indicates that he understands what he has been studying. If he has mispronounced words, or his language has been grammatically incorrect, corrections may be made afterward. I have heard pupils recite history and other lessons verbatim, when they had no idea whatever of the meaning of the words they were repeating.

Another direction to pupils in close connection with the last is to give every answer in a complete sentence. If they have the thought, they should be able to give entire expression to it. In no other way can their knowledge of a lesson or subject be thoroughly tested.

Pupils must not "prompt" or assist one another. Each must depend upon himself if he would get the benefit to be derived from the recitation.

They may raise hands, provided, first, that no one is speaking—politeness requires the observance of this rule; secondly, when they can answer; thirdly, when they can add to an answer; fourthly, when they wish to criticise; fifthly, when they wish to ask a question; sixthly, when they wish to communicate with another pupil.

They should always speak in low tones, not too rapidly, and always distinctly.

DIRECTIONS TO TEACHERS.

The last direction to pupils applies to teachers as well, for how can they expect pupils to speak in low tones of voice, slowly and distinctly, if they do not themselves set the example?

Neither should the teacher "prompt" in recitation or examination, though the temptation to do so is very great. "Prompting" another destroys self-confidence and degrades self-respect. It is an unkind act, however well intentioned. The sooner the pupil learns that self-help is the best help, the better it is for him.

The teacher should be polite to pupils. It always pays. One point I would insist upon is, that no teacher should ever address a pupil by his surname without prefixing a title. It is both coarse and rude. In addressing a young lady, the title "Miss" should be prefixed to the surname. In speaking to a young gentleman, speak to him in a respectful manner, using the title "Mr." or "Master." In the case of younger pupils you may use their given names, but the manner should never be other than polite. Politeness, even to the verge of formality, does not weaken the authority of a teacher, but strengthens it by securing and retaining the respect of pupils.

Do not repeat questions. This habit on the part of a teacher encourages carelessness and inattention on the part of pupils.

Do not repeat answers. It is not necessary; it wastes time, and makes the teacher appear like an echoing machine.

Govern yourself; do not get angry. Never let pupils see that you are annoyed. Nothing so delights mischievous or vicious pupils so much as to see that they can annoy the teacher, and they are quick to follow up an advantage thus gained. Woe to the teacher who thus places herself at the mercy of "young tyrants"!

Govern your own pupils. Do not show weakness by asking the principal or school-board to come to your assistance unless in a great emergency. The teacher who is continually referring cases of discipline to the principal or board can not long maintain control of her pupils.

Again, a teacher or person in charge of a schoolroom is supposed to be able to manage it, and all communications to or by any one in it should be made through her or by her permission. No person has a right to disregard this rule, whether a pupil or other person.

Should a superintendent, director, or any one in real

authority, even over the person in charge, wish to cross the room, or to address any one in it, he has no right to do so without first being recognized by, and obtaining permission from, the person in charge. The proper influences can not be exerted in a school where the rights of all are not duly respected.

Teachers should take care of their health, and bring vigor of body and mind to the recitation.

They should always prepare the lesson. Even if it is a simple subject, the teacher should know just what is in it, and the ideas of the author of the text-book used. He should know just how he intends teaching it, and how to meet and explain difficulties apt to arise in the minds of the pupils. The teacher who thinks there is nothing to be done but "grind out the lesson of the day by asking a few set questions" and listening to the corresponding answers has much to learn. New fields are opening all the time, and teachers must keep abreast of the times if they would succeed. There is a spirit to be brought out, developed, in the boys and girls. It is for the teacher to arouse and direct the energies of her pupils, so that they will become interested, and do their best in every recitation.

The words and acts of teachers should be such as to honor their profession.

Methods of Conducting Recitations.
1. Oral.
    a. Individual.
        1. Consecutive.   2. Promiscuous.
    b. Concert.
    c. Questions and answers.
    d. Topical.
    e. Lectures.
    f. Discussions.
    g. Reciprocal.
2. Written.
3. Oral and written.
    a. Diagrams.
    b. Outlines.

Directions to Pupils
1. Stand or sit erect.
2. Obey signals.
    a. Promptly.
    b. Quietly.
3. Be polite.
    a. To teachers.
    b. To one another.
    c. To everybody.
4. Give answers.
    a. In your own words.
    b. In complete sentences.
5. Do not prompt.
6. Raise hands—when
    a. No one is speaking.
    b. You can answer.
    c. You can add to answer.
    d. You wish to criticise.
    e. You wish to ask a question.
    f. You wish to communicate with any one.
7. Speak.
    a. In low tones.
    b. Slowly.
    c. Distinctly.

Directions to Teachers.

1. Speak.
    a. In low tones.
    b. Slowly.
    c. Distinctly.
2. Do not prompt.
    a. In recitation.
    b. In examination.
3. Be polite to pupils.
4. Do not repeat.
    a. Questions.
    b. Answers.
5. Govern yourself.
6. Govern your own pupils.
7. Prepare for recitation.
8. Let all your acts and words be worthy of your profession.
9. Be
    a. Original.
    b. Enthusiastic.
    c. Energetic.
    d. Spirited.
    e. Systematic.
    f. Kind.
    g. Cheerful.
    h. Firm.
    i. Self-possessed.
    k. Dignified.
    l. Patient.

CHAPTER V.

LENGTH OF RECITATION.

In this chapter will be considered the length of recitation, the assignment and preparation of lessons, and criticism.

A recitation should not continue too long; neither should it be too short. If it is too long, pupils grow weary, the teacher can not hold their attention, and the advantages of the recitation are lost; if the recitation is too short, the subject of the lesson can not be properly discussed or understood. In colleges, recitations are usually about an hour in length; in high and normal schools, from thirty to forty minutes; and in graded and ungraded schools they vary from ten to thirty minutes in length, being ten, fifteen, or twenty minutes in primary rooms. In looking over a programme recently, I observed that the teacher had arranged it so as to give ten minutes daily to the most advanced grade in arithmetic, ten minutes to United States history, ten minutes to the class in physical geography, and ten minutes to the primary class. He had arranged for a certain number of classes, and thought he must give the same length of time to the beginners that he gave to advanced pupils, and that every recitation should be just ten minutes long. "Now," said he, "the people can not complain, for I give as much time to the little children as I do to the large boys and girls." This programme was published in the newspapers to show the particular work of the teacher in the schoolroom. It might at first appear to be just, because of the equable division of time. But, when we come to examine the subject carefully, most of us would agree in pronouncing it unjust. And why? Let us consider it in this light. Little children can not control their attention for a great length of time, hence their recitations should be short, lest they grow weary and learn nothing. With larger children, who have learned to keep the attention longer under control of the will, and who have learned how to study a new subject understandingly, it is quite different. They are better prepared for recitation, and can bear extended criticism and the questioning and cross-questioning of the teacher and classmates better than little children. For this reason it is quite evident that the length of a recitation for small children should never be more than fifteen minutes.

In the higher grades of ward-schools, and the advanced classes of ungraded schools, thirty minutes may be profitably given to recitations, but never more. In a normal or a high school, forty minutes should be the limit of length of recitation. The two extremes must be avoided. Time enough should be given to have all the points in a lesson brought out and understood, but in no case should the recitation be continued so long that pupils lose their interest in the subject.

The length of the recitation determined, the division

of the time is of importance. Since every lesson is connected with the one preceding it, five or ten minutes should be taken for review.

Suppose the recitation to be one in general history. History is a continuous stream; it is not simply the life of an individual, but of humanity; and we look upon all humanity as passing down the current of time. We study that stream from its source. We look back over thousands of years into the early ages, or we glance forward a thousand years into the future, and we discover that everything is related to something else— every event to some other event. This relationship is not only true in history, but equally true of the facts in the sciences, whether of the natural sciences or the sciences of political and social economy. The time set apart for review will give opportunity to discuss this. Then allow ten or fifteen minutes for the blackboard work. Dividing the class into sections corresponding in number to the number of topics in the lesson, let the pupils pass to the board and write outlines of the topics. That done, the remainder of the time well improved will be ample for oral recitation upon these topics, and for the introduction of general information gathered by pupils from outside sources which they think may have some relation to the subject of the lesson. This relationship, if existing, may be shown; or, if their judgment is in error, the error may be made to appear, and their mental faculties receive additional culture by this.

For illustration, one teacher required all the pupils in his room to write each week the new facts learned during the preceding week. On one occasion some of the pupils brought in notes upon the trouble between

China and France, while others had been writing about "comet dust," supposed to have been the cause of the red light seen evenings and mornings in the sky; still others had been investigating the proceedings of "the Court of Inquiry," and others had followed out a line of railroad between two cities remote from each other. It is possible to bring to bear upon a historical question a great many facts, and the relationship of a railroad to the history and development of the country through which it passes may be shown to have a bearing upon the lesson of the day.

The teacher who is no broader than a text-book is narrow indeed. He should understand a subject so thoroughly that, if the text-book were lost, he could teach as well without it as with it. In the German schools the teacher must be able to stand before his classes and conduct his recitations without the aid of text-books, and, if necessary, throw additional light on any point not fully presented by the author. Each subject should be taught as though the teacher were a specialist in that subject.

You know what Emerson's views were upon successful teaching. In teaching, as in everything else, the secret of success is inspiration; and the inspired teacher can get pupils to know their own ability to do something. In a primary-school not long since, I saw a good illustration of this. There were many of the children so small that they could not put on their overcoats. The teacher arranged the children in platoons, and the larger children assisted the smaller ones. Many primary teachers complain of having to dress and undress the children. This teacher had found a way out of the difficulty. She directed the children, and they did the work.

Assignment of Lessons.

It is important that lessons be properly assigned and carefully prepared. Much progress has been made in the last few years in this department of educational work, and, in order to give the reader an idea of how things have been done in some old-time schools, I will tell the story of an ambitious boy who studied arithmetic under difficulties. He had studied reading and spelling for some time, when the teacher, in a gracious mood, said to him one day, "George, I think you are big enough to cipher." George, very much elated, ran home as soon as school was out and told his father what the teacher had said. His father was delighted, and promised to get a slate and an arithmetic for him. This promise he sacredly kept, and the next morning George was the happy owner of a slate of immense proportions, and a copy of Smith's arithmetic. He felt grand indeed as he entered the door of the old log school-house at the end of the lane. He showed his new property to the teacher, who gave him his first exercise in arithmetic. The teacher said, "If you have one apple in your right hand, and another apple in your left hand, how many apples have you in both?" Could such an exercise ever be forgotten? George solved that problem, and, happy in the knowledge that he might have two apples, turned over a leaf or two in the book and came to the addition table, which he committed to memory, and then worked on as fast as he could through addition, subtraction, multiplication, and division. No lesson was ever assigned by the teacher, but he simply worked out each day as many problems as he could. Whenever his slate was full he showed it to the teacher, who would say, "Very well done," and, with a shy glance at the slate covered with figures, hand it back as quickly as possible. He never had a recitation. When he came to a problem too difficult for him, he took it to the teacher, who solved it (if he could). In the same school, in the reading lessons, each one read a "verse," as it was called, the teacher correcting the mistakes in pronunciation. Whenever the teacher did assign a lesson in anything, it was assigned by pages, never by topic.

The lesson assigned should be as much as the average pupil can learn well. Care should be taken not to give too much, and thus discourage pupils, nor too little, but enough to require earnest effort on the part of the pupil to master it.

There should be a definite time for taking up and studying a subject, and a definite time for laying it aside. At no time and on no account should a teacher go beyond the minute, or allow a pupil to do so. The order of exercises should be so distinctly understood by the pupils that they know when to prepare every subject as well as when to recite it. To enable them to meet this requirement, the programme should be placed on the blackboard where all can see it.

To recapitulate. The important points in assigning a lesson are:

First. Assign subjects rather than pages.

Secondly. Assign as much as the class can well prepare.

Thirdly. Let the lesson be a little too short rather than too long.

Fourthly. Instruct the pupil as to *how* you wish the lesson prepared.

The last is a very important point.

Should you wish to teach pupils how to commit to memory, select a sentence for example the following: "With regard to the origin of the cause, there has been the greatest diversity of opinion." Read it slowly through—once, twice, three times, as many times as you think necessary—and close the book; then try to reproduce the sentence from memory, thinking carefully about it, and referring to the book if necessary. Explain to the pupils, in words, the process, showing them, by the use of terms simple enough for their comprehension, that we commit to memory by repetition—that iteration is a law of memory.

It has been asserted that more pupils fail in arithmetic from the fact that they do not understand the language than from any difficulty there may be in the subject itself. The teacher must be sure that they get the idea, and then illustrate to them the process of expressing the idea. In arithmetic this is done by the solution and explanation of a problem, using the rule that is given as a guide. Having read the problem carefully through, do with it just what the rule directs, taking one step at a time, and describing it fully as it is taken. The problems and rules fall under certain general principles, the use of which children should be taught to understand, and not required to commit to memory. The rule is like a sign-post, showing which way to go; but definitions should be committed to memory by the process already indicated, when the language is fully understood. In every definition there is what may be called the "key-word," without which the definition loses its force, and this very word is often the one children are inclined to omit. A little care on the part of the teacher will teach the children to look for the "key-word," and the learning of definitions will not be very difficult. As an illustration, take the definition of the "greatest common divisor"; omit the word "greatest" in it, and the whole definition is wrecked.

In teaching children how to study, impress upon their minds the value of cheerful, earnest study. Insist upon cheerful faces, and set the example yourself, even though behind your own apparently cheerful face there linger traces of care, of anxiety, of illness. The very effort to appear cheerful drives away much of the hidden pain, and the children should not be permitted to suffer because the teacher suffers. If she is irritable, they become so; if she suffers, they suffer; for they are sympathetic, are imitative, and any disturbing element hinders progress in their school-work. Lively, pleasant manners in the teacher are indispensable to success.

How to deal with those who are unprepared for recitation is a most perplexing question. What should be done with a boy who will not prepare the lessons? It should be so managed that he will feel the loss. He may be sent home; it is his loss. But there may be reasons to justify his failure; there may be sickness at home, or misfortune of some kind. It is still his loss, for a class can not be kept back for the sake of one pupil. The only thing at present recommended is that he be held responsible for the discovery of the lost points in the subject; he must find the means for his own relief. A wide-awake, industrious teacher can make such use of the time spent in the discussion of the general information topics, and their relation to the subject of the lesson, as to compel the pupils to feel that they can not afford to lose a single recitation or any part of it.

CRITICISM

is not simply fault-finding, pointing out errors; it is judging, and applies to the separation of errors from truths. Wholesome criticism is necessary, but commendation should be given when deserved. Now comes the question, "Who should criticise?" I think that, in advanced classes particularly, the pupils should be the first to do this. If their criticisms are correct and exhaust the subject, the teacher has little to do beyond presiding and supervising. If any important points have been omitted, the teacher should call attention to them.

How to criticise is more important than who should do it. The object of criticism must be kept in view, and the criticisms, though just in pointing out errors, may be so made as to defeat the object. To illustrate: Superintendents sometimes criticise teachers. This is the way in which it was done on one occasion: The superintendent was a man of very determined will. He went into the room of a teacher whom he did not admire very much, although he found her doing as well as she could. He was not pleased with the exercises, and said to her, "That is wrong; do it this way; do it that way," in a sharp, angry tone of voice. This confused her so that she began to weep. His manner shocked the pupils. They sympathized with their teacher. The criticism was unjust, because of its manner and the place in which it was made. He should have spoken to the teacher privately, or have written memoranda and made suggestions for her guidance. He should have spoken in the proper spirit and in a kindly manner. Instead of bluntly saying "That is wrong," it is better to say, "I think that, perhaps, you would find some other way preferable to that," and explain that *other way*.

There is much in knowing how to present a subject, how to criticise without giving offense. One of the most learned men of the times softens his criticism by giving it as his mere opinion. He says "*I think* it is this way." Every one who hears him knows that he is correct in the statement that he makes, and that he *knows* that he is correct; and yet he speaks as if he might possibly be in error, to avoid giving offense. Remember—criticise so as not to offend.

As a summary of thoughts on criticism we give:

First. Let pupils criticise.

Secondly. The teacher should notice omissions in criticisms made by pupils.

Thirdly. The teacher should commend pupils for whatever is well done. This stimulates to renewed exertions.

Fourthly. Criticisms properly made are remembered and suggestions acted upon. There is no need of repeating them.

CHAPTER VI.

ART OF QUESTIONING.

1. GENERAL methods of questioning.
2. Personal questioning.
3. Questioning pupils.
4. Pupils questioning one another.
5. Book questioning.

The great questioner of all ages was Socrates, the Grecian philosopher. Socrates, as a philosopher, sought not so much to establish the truth of a statement of philosophy dogmatically, as to involve persons by apt questioning, make them entrap themselves, and thus lead them to see the defects of their definitions.

For instance, if a definition was asserted to be true, Socrates questioned in his own mind whether the assertion was correct, and then, in conversation with the person who made the statement, he would seek, by a series of questions, to involve him in contradiction, perhaps in several contradictions, and show, by his methods of questioning, that the statement was not true, but false. Hence originated that method which has been handed down to us from ancient times, and which we call the Socratic method. I would recommend to those interested in the *art* of questioning the study of some of the dialogues in which Socrates was the questioner. Not that those examples pertain particularly to school work, but to show the skill with which he put his questions. At the present time, those persons who question most adroitly, and whose business it is to test the truthfulness of certain propositions, are found in the legal profession. Lawyers, especially those noted for their skill in the cross-examination of witnesses, adopt the methods of Socrates. Not alone in the legal profession, however, but in that of teaching, is there afforded a fine field for the display of ability in the art of questioning.

It has been already stated that the pupil must learn for himself; that the teacher can only guide him in certain lines of thought. The art of questioning correctly is in strict harmony with this proposition. Pupils are not always so questioned as to develop their mental faculties. Hence, for a full discussion of the subject, I have suggested the above outline: First, the general methods of questioning; secondly, personal questioning —that is, questions that the pupils should ask themselves, or that the teacher should ask himself; thirdly, questioning pupils, in which the teacher displays whatever ability he may possess; fourthly, pupils questioning either the teacher or one another; fifthly, book questioning.

GENERAL QUESTIONING.

Much of the work in the school-room is carried on by questions and answers. The methods are either oral or written, or a combination of them. With beginners the exercises are almost exclusively oral. A written question should have but one meaning, and that so clearly stated that no mistake could possibly occur. In preparing questions of either kind, the teacher ought to keep the objective point prominently in view. By gradual steps the pupil is conducted to a certain height, as it were, whence he is enabled to recall the successive efforts put forth to reach it. A series of questions, beginning with what a pupil knows, and so fitted together that each question depends upon all that precedes it and builds upon that, is an educational appliance which any teacher may be proud to invent, but which can not be secured without close and careful application and a quick insight into the varying moods of the human mind. Whether a teacher should ask oral or written questions, depends upon circumstances.

It is conceded that oral questions enable a teacher to make his work tell, and to inspire his pupils with genuine enthusiasm. There is an electric shock from the eye and an inspiration from the voice which stimulate pupils to do their best. But a languid and sleepy eye, a weak, undecided, and faltering voice, no matter how excellent the teacher's other qualifications may be, will disorganize any school and spoil the pupils.

Let the questions be so put that they will bring out, or suggest, ideas to the pupils, and that they enable them to arrange what knowledge they possess in a systematic manner. Random, incoherent questions are to be avoided while trying to fix an idea in a pupil's mind. One thought well grounded is of more value than a dozen others only partially understood.

PERSONAL QUESTIONS.

The following questions are suggestive to the teacher preparing for a recitation:

1. What does this lesson contain?
2. Is it adapted to the pupils studying it?
3. How much time will be required by the pupils in its preparation?
4. Am I thoroughly prepared to conduct this exercise?
5. How is it related to what precedes it?
6. How is it related to what follows it?
7. What new material is needed with which to illustrate it?
8. Shall the children furnish the illustrations, or shall I furnish them?
9. How is this subject related to other subjects in this book?
10. How shall I show these relations?
11. What are the natural divisions of this subject?
12. Can I induce the pupils to find out the divisions for themselves?
13. Shall I use the analytic or the synthetic method, or shall I use both methods in presenting this subject to the pupils?
14. What difficulties are the pupils most apt to have in mastering it?
15. What faculties of the mind are exercised in learning this lesson?
16. Are any members of my class deficient in these faculties? How can they be developed?

17. How can the knowledge gained from this lesson be utilized in after life?

18. In what respects are my methods defective?

19. How can I improve?

20. Is my language such that my pupils can understand?

21. Do I speak in a loud, harsh, grating voice?

22. If so, what effect does my talking have upon my pupils?

23. Do I pronounce correctly all the words that I use?

PERSONAL QUESTIONS FOR EACH PUPIL.

1. Do I comply with all just requirements in school?
2. Do I give entire attention to my work?
3. Am I always honest?
4. Am I always polite?
5. Do I connect what I learn each day with what I had previously known?
6. Can I apply the knowledge I have gained to the every-day affairs of life?

PUPILS QUESTIONING.

Pupils should be encouraged to ask questions—that is, proper questions. When Des Cartes, the celebrated philosopher, was a boy and went to school, he continually tormented his teachers with questions, and was called the "boy philosopher." He has since then tormented the world with questions. It is often said that little children will ask questions that the wisest can not answer. This spirit (or faculty) of asking questions needs to be cultivated in the right direction, otherwise it becomes offensive.

In intermediate and higher grades, when a pupil makes a statement or explains a problem, if he be forced to defend his assertions and demonstrations against the adverse criticisms of his classmates, he is taught a practical lesson in cautiousness which will save him many mistakes in after life, and create in him that habit of mind which is called by some writers, *judicial*. Such criticism, properly conducted, has a strong tendency to keep this point clearly before the mind of the pupil, namely, *to give a good reason for what he believes. This is the everlasting "why"* which presses upon every rational being.

If you wish to know the difficulties pupils have with a lesson they are trying to master, you must know how the subject appears to them; you must understand them; put yourself in their places; see from their standpoint. Very well did that novelist express it when he said "Put yourself in his place." If he had never written anything else but that title to his book, he would have suggested a volume in that one short sentence. Teachers must learn to see a subject as their pupils see it, and keep in mind that children are not empty vessels to have knowledge poured into them.

BOOK QUESTIONS.

Book questions are good for that class of teachers called out in the West "reciting-posts." On the banks of the Mississippi River there are posts to which rafts are hitched by ropes, and then pulled slowly to shore. Some teachers use the "book questions" exclusively. These questions serve but as the ropes, and children, like the rafts, are held, simply drifting till they get through the book from the first page to the last.

The time has come when the best teachers are those who ask four or five questions not on the page for every question there. The tendency of recent years is toward cultivating independence of thought on the part of pupils, and to give them power to question for themselves, and to see what questions should be asked and answered.

APPLICATION.

Success in the art of questioning pupils consists in asking such questions that they must answer freely and independently without prompting or assisting. The questions should in no way suggest the answers. I know that many teachers are strongly tempted to "prompt" pupils who are anxious to answer the questions correctly. But it is far better for the pupil that he be not "prompted," but rely entirely upon himself. The *art* of questioning a pupil properly consists in asking such questions as will test his knowledge of the subject, and not in making a display of the teacher's knowledge.

Suppose you ask a pupil to tell you the differences between a noun and a pronoun, and he tells you as many of the differences as he can think of. You then ask another pupil to tell you in what respects they are alike, and he tells you all the agreements he can think of between them. Each answers in his own language, and in complete sentences. Then, after all have answered, if there is anything additional that you can think of, you try to bring it out by asking questions—

such questions as make the pupils think out what is desired.

Ask questions like these: "In what respects are decimal and common fractions alike? In what respects do they differ?" Do not "prompt them." Let them tell you all they know about it. When one gets through reciting, correct his language or make suggestions if necessary. Do not allow pupils to throw up their hands as soon as a question is asked, or when a mistake is made. This is one of the ways of "prompting" practiced in schools. Let the pupils wait, as has been suggested before, till the person reciting gets through or is excused. Then, if they have corrections to make, let them raise their hands. It is said that in some of the Scotch schools, when a question is asked, all the pupils of the class rush toward the teacher with hands up, all wanting to speak at once.

In questioning children, the skillful teacher asks questions adapted to them, comes down to the plane they occupy, gets them to tell what they know, sets them to thinking, and leads them to see the relation between the starting-point and that which he wishes them to reach in the circumference of their knowledge. It is in the questioning of pupils that the teacher needs most to be an *artist*.

The first educational work I ever read was that grand book on the "Theory and Practice of Teaching," by David Page. It is a book that every teacher should read. It was that book which first opened up to my mind the fact that there was anything in the work of education above the mere hearing of classes. It was the inspiration of that book while I taught my second country school that gave an impetus to my whole life. I read of the two trees — the straight tree and the crooked tree; and, when I had learned how difficult it is to straighten a crooked tree, I felt that, as a teacher, I had a higher, more important work to do than simply to ask set questions and listen to the answers given by pupils in the words of the book. When I read that chapter in which is discussed the subject of asking questions, and in which he tells about visiting a school and hearing a recitation in mental arithmetic, I looked about among my acquaintances, and found that nearly all the teachers I knew were following the same method that was there portrayed in such glowing language.

TOO MUCH HELP—ANECDOTES.

Visiting a school not long since, I found a class of children that were reading about "*a child.*" They were bright but noisy children. Having heard the subject announced, I was curious to know just what line the teacher would pursue, since it did not exactly state whether the child was "a boy or a girl." However, the teacher struck out as follows:

"How many think the child was a girl?" No time was given for an answer. "How many think it was a boy?" No time for answer. "How many think it might be either a boy or a girl?" No time for answer. "How many think it was either a boy or a girl?" No answer, but a few raised their hands. "How many are positive one way or the other?" A few hands raised, but still no answer. "How many believe it might have been?" Then a pause, but the hands did not go up. "Now, what shall we say about it?" There were no hands raised, but they were getting ready. Then John said, "I don't know." That was the first answer. "Yes, that's all right. We will now go on," said the teacher.

At another time a friend invited me to visit a school in the country. The teacher had told me that the pupils in his school understood mental arithmetic better than the pupils in city schools. I was quite willing to go and ascertain the truthfulness of his statement for myself. One of the school directors of that district went with me. We had been in the room but a few moments before I came to the conclusion that it must be the same school that David Page had visited forty years before. In order to show off the class, three girls were called out to recite in mental arithmetic. They were using a book which is used in many schools. One of the problems given was this: "If $\frac{2}{4}$ of a certain number is 12, what is that number?" They were ready for recitation. The teacher gave the question slowly and distinctly, and then said, "Mary will answer." Mary said, "Well, if $\frac{2}{4}$ of a certain number is 12, what is that number?" "Now, Mary, you have first to find $\frac{2}{4}$?" "Yes." "Well, $\frac{2}{4}$ of 12 is 4?" "Yes." "No, no, no, no; now watch again. If $\frac{2}{4}$ of a certain number is 12, what are you to find?" "Well, I am to find the number." After he got through, he looked around with a triumphant air. "Well," I said to him, "will you please let me ask the girls a question?" "Certainly." I said, "If 15 is $\frac{2}{4}$ of a certain number, what is that number?" He answered three questions before I could get the attention of the girls to one, and would persist in helping them. I asked the teacher to let the girls answer, but he would interrupt, and commenced: "Now, you want $\frac{1}{5}$ of 15?" "Yes." "Now what is 4 times 5?"

A CONTRAST.

I visited another school, the teacher of which is one of the most successful in the art of questioning I ever knew. When I entered his room but one pupil was out of order, judging by the most fastidious standard adopted in schools. That one boy was not sitting just in line. The teacher was conducting a language exercise, and asked the pupils to write sentences using the words *meet* and *meat*. Two points were to be observed: both the words must be used in one sentence, and the sentence must be written in good English. One boy wrote, "I will meet my father after I buy the meat." The class agreed that the sentence fulfilled the conditions. The decision of the teacher was not required.

CHAPTER VII.

TEACHING READING.

There are a few important preliminaries which can not be omitted without detriment to the pupil who is learning how to read. The pupil should be taught how to sit and how to stand so as to give his vocal organs and his respiratory organs free, easy, and natural action. He should sit or stand erect, hold his chin down near his throat, breathe through his nose, keep the muscles of the neck and face relaxed, shoulders thrown backward and slightly downward, stand firmly on one or both of his feet, hold the book at a convenient distance from the eyes, so that both eyes see the words under the same visual angle. He must also be taught how to inhale and how to exhale air, as well as how to economize his breath in reading and convert it into sound. So far this work is mechanical, and it has reference to the pupil as a machine capable of running without friction or danger of breakage, but without such attention liable to accidents of the gravest character. Just as the human voice is an instrument of the most wonderful powers, and susceptible of the highest degree of improvement and perfection, so is it important that it, with the breathing apparatus, should be developed in a rational and harmonious manner.

In order to teach reading well, the teacher must know what are natural, pure tones of voice, and how to develop such qualities of voice in the pupils, provided their tones are defective in any manner. The human voice, in one sense, is an instrument possessing the most delicate and wonderful properties in regard to quality, form, pitch, force, rate, and stress. A teacher whose ear is not trained to detect the harsh and discordant tones that children sometimes employ, and, even after detecting them, does not know how to remedy them, is unfit for teaching reading. We might as well commit the care of the sick to that pretended physician whose recommendation to practice medicine is a stolen diploma from some printing-office, and who does not know disease from health.

An experienced reader will at once detect any impurity in the quality of the voice, and in drilling he knows just how to correct it. If a child does not know the multiplication-table, his progress in arithmetic is slow indeed, and if he is allowed to continue his faulty methods in reading, and the teacher does not see them, or is ignorant of the treatment the case requires, the result will be worse than zero.

Reading is the most important, as well as the most difficult, branch to teach in the entire course of instruction—the most important, because the most used and the most necessary; and the most difficult, because the least understood and appreciated. It is the first study of the child at school, and the one that he uses daily ever after. It is very properly denominated "the key to all knowledge," hence the reason it should be correctly taught in all grades, but more particularly in the primary. If neglected here, the probabilities are that the pupil will never become a good reader.

To show that it is not appreciated, we have but to refer to those occupying public places whose vocal delivery is anything but pleasing, and whose reading is simply outrageous. Even many who have graduated from the best institutions in the land have entirely neglected that culture which would enable them to read appropriately a section from a statute, an extract from the Bible, or a hymn for a congregation. These persons are careful in the use of language, written and spoken, frequently refer to the dictionary for correct pronunciation, and would be only too willing to acquire a full, round, musical tone of voice, so as to read and speak with grace, propriety, and ease. But too late in life they discover that one essential part of their education has been sadly neglected.

It is not in public only that good reading exerts an influence; it may be in the highest degree a source of pleasure and instruction in the home circle. A good book, read aloud at home, not only disseminates useful knowledge, but is a power in the formation of character. How important, then, that our school-children should be taught correctly in this branch, which, above all others, is the universal branch of education!

We will endeavor to test every step in the discussion of the subject before us—teaching reading by the educational principles which have been already presented. At this time there is a general awakening in reference to teaching reading to all grades of pupils. A prominent educator has made this definition: "Reading is getting and giving thought by means of written or printed words arranged in sentences."

An excellent teacher, who had given much thought to the subject, defined it as follows: "Reading is the process of conveying ideas from a manuscript or book to our own minds or to the minds of others."

"Elocution," according to Mr. Hamill, "is the science of expressing thought and feeling by utterance and action." These definitions are worthy to be remembered, compared, analyzed. Do this, and then make definitions of your own if they are not satisfactory.

Since a large majority of children attend school only a few years at most, there is an urgent necessity for correct instruction early in life, and especially so in teaching reading to primary classes.

In all instruction the teacher should keep in view the fact that the pupil is soon to *help himself*, and in imparting instruction in reading—the foundation-study—this principle should not for a moment be lost sight of. The child must become a self-reliant worker, not a mere imitator. With this in view, each lesson should exercise the perceptive faculties, the imagination, the taste, and the judgment.

The *sum of all reasons why reading should* be correctly taught is this: Upon correct reading—namely, getting the sense out of what is printed or written—depends every other acquisition.

Reading resolves itself into certain distinct elements which the teacher must observe: 1. Foremost is the object. 2. The processes. 3. The principles. 4. Application of the principles. 5. The child and the kind of culture that his nature requires. 6. The literary selections adapted to each class.

In what precedes, the object of reading has been pointed out, and it need not be repeated.

As to processes, there are many, and they go by different names. The teacher is stumbling over them almost every day. Perhaps the most ancient and venerable method is that known as the "A B C method," once in vogue, but now retired from active service. A few strong authorities still indorse it. They advocate it because it goes away back to first principles—straight and curved lines. It has age in its favor, but, in my opinion, no other recommendation.

Ideas are first awakened in the mind by impressions made on some one or more of the senses. We do not know how these impressions are transformed into ideas, but the transformation does occur, nevertheless. The second step is this: The idea in the mind must be expressed through the medium called language. Reading, therefore, consists in giving expression to the ideas the mind has formed.

If the ideas be false or inadequate, the expression of them will be correspondingly false.

The methods yet to be discussed proceed upon the hypothesis that the child has something in his mind which he wants to express, and that the teacher stands by to help him to tell it properly. The second method is the "word method." This method consists in taking some familiar object, as a "hat," and then letting the children talk about it to the teacher. In due time the teacher calls attention to the spoken word, "hat," and finally to the printed or written word, "hat." The children soon learn the connection between the spoken word and the printed or written word, and they may also know how to spell the word by letter and also by sound as well as how to write it. The essential point in this method is that the pupil learns to know a word by its looks, and upon the same principle that he learns to know a cat from a cap. It is even claimed that a child may learn two or three hundred words in this way, before he knows a single letter of the alphabet. Reading under such conditions is naming the words with correct expression.

Observe, first, the idea; secondly, the expression of the idea. The manner of expressing the idea is reading. It is impossible for a pupil to express his ideas clearly and intelligibly unless he first feels that he has something to say, and knows how to say it.

As will be observed, the unit is the word, and there must be as many elements or different words to learn by sight, if the vocabulary be an exhaustive one, as there are words in the reading-book the pupil uses.

Another method is that known as the "sentence method." The sentence is the unit. The pupil learns a sentence by its looks. A string of words to him is a sentence, and, hearing the sentence read, he attaches a meaning to the sentence as he understands it, and then he tries to connect the spoken with the written or printed sentence. Repeating the sentence with different modulations of the voice will enable the pupil to observe and practice those turns or slides of the voice which add so much to the beauty of vocal delivery. It is also claimed that pupils may learn a large number of sentences without even finding out the separate words composing them, yet it hardly appears credible, owing to the well-known disposition of children to tear things to pieces. Of course the advocates of this method claim superior advantages in its favor.

If we consider the sentence as the unit of thought, then, naturally, the word is the unit of language, and the letter is the unit of words. Whether the teacher employs the "word method" or the "sentence method," the idea precedes the word or the sentence. The thing itself goes before the sign. Words and sentences are visible or oral expressions for ideas already in the mind.

Again, the clearer the concept is in the pupil's mind, the better will he express himself. If the reading be of such a nature as not to add any new thought to the thoughts the pupil already has, then his work is valueless. To add to the intellectual acquisitions of the mind is to combine simple concepts into more complex ones, and that study which does not furnish such material as is readily assimilated by combination must be classed low in the scale of mental culture.

Now, the starting-point in any system of reading must depend, first, upon the idea in the mind, and, secondly, upon how to express that idea in such tones of voice as the sense indicates. Reading viewed from this elevated standpoint offers the very best field for the exercise of all the higher faculties of the mind, as well as for arousing into vigorous activity the entire emotional nature. Indeed, I do not know of any other branch in the entire curriculum of studies that appeals so powerfully to every faculty of the human soul, nor do I know of any other subject that in general is so poorly taught. The voice is something that needs culture, and, if impure tones have been acquired, the teacher ought to know how to correct them at once. If no bad habits of voice have been contracted, the voice needs cultivation to give it smoothness, volume, intensity, and compass. Naturally, the child-voice is pure, and it is by gross negligence or mismanagement that impure qualities of voice are fostered.

An experienced musician detects instantly the slightest discord—even the country singing-school master can tell whether all his pupils sing the same note; but, positively, there are thousands of "school-keepers" who are unable to point out as glaring mistakes in reading as a failure to sing the scale correctly would be in vocal music.

PHONIC METHOD.

This method as such differs from the others. The names of the letters are not spoken, the sounds only being taught. Take the word "hat." A is simply sounded as ă. The whole word may be analyzed by giving the sound of each letter. The teacher should give each sound first. letting the child repeat it. To get the sound of ă, let the child speak the word "ăt" after the teacher, slowly, and then begin to say the word and leave it unfinished, not giving the sound of "t." By such practice as this phonic analysis is easily learned, and the relation between the sound and the name of a letter is soon established.

A teacher who will show to her class the exact position and movements of the vocal organs, with a little special explanation in individual cases, will be astonished to discover that very little time will be required to teach a class to give all the sounds accurately. Those teachers who have difficulty in distinguishing or giving the sounds can, by studying the positions of the vocal organs, conquer the most difficult sounds or combination of sounds. To illustrate: take the long sound of "ā," which any one can give, and notice the position of the lips, tongue, and the mouth. From that sound of ā go at once to the short sound ă, watching in a looking-glass, if necessary, the change in position of the mouth, until you are familiar with the process, and can explain in words those elements of the change which the children can not see. Some positions of the vocal organs close the mouth, so that the children can learn to make the correct sounds only by imitation and practice.

Whether children learn to read at first by the *word, sentence,* or *phonic method,* they soon learn the names of the letters. At least this has been my experience, and it is a fruitless waste of time to adopt subterfuges in order to avoid teaching the names of the letters. Only a few persons ever had any trouble in learning the names of the letters, and most of them learned their letters so easily that they have forgotten when and how they did learn them.

As I understand the method of Colonel Parker, formerly of Quincy, he uses no book at first, but, with the children before him, takes a familiar object and talks with the children about it till they become interested in it. He then draws a picture of the object on the board, and from this picture the children draw one on their slates. The name of the object is written beneath it in a large, bold hand. All the letters are written unusually large. When the word is written underneath the picture, the children have made the distinction between the object and the picture, and also between the spoken word and the written word, and, since all progress in the acquisition of knowledge depends upon the ability of the pupil to point out agreements and differences, it is readily perceived that this method has many excellent features to commend it. But Mr. Parker has the children learn to read script first. The philosophy for this I can not discover. The teacher writes the reading-lessons for beginners on the board. They see it produced by her own hand, and it is claimed that this gives it a freshness and a personal inspiration that are wanting in the printed form. It is also a fact that children will readily change from the written to the printed form without loss of time. The transition either way is easy.

The skillful teacher is not a person of any one method, but a person of methods; able, as it were, to take the good out of all, and combine it into a working system of her own.

There is no valid reason, so far as I can discover, why the child from the first should not spell all the words in his lessons by letter and by sound. He must learn the names of the letters as well as the sounds, and it will require only a few days for the child of ordinary intelligence to learn both.

JACOTOT'S METHOD.

While this method is particularly adapted to acquiring a knowledge of a language unknown to the learner, it is so suggestive in other respects that I refer to it in order to show the resources of a teacher who stands in the foremost rank of the great educators. M. Jacotot, a Frenchman, in 1818, was called to teach pupils who were Hollanders. He did not know one word of the Dutch language, and they did not know one word of the French language. Here was a problem. I met a similar case in a northern city while visiting schools there a few years since. A young lady who had been reared in the South had secured a position in a part of the city settled by Germans, whose children could not speak a word of English. She could not speak a word of German, and so she sang to them at first.

But mark what M. Jacotot did. He took as the text-book the French classic, "Telemaque." It was in French, but with an interlinear translation in Dutch written under the French. He had to give his instruction to the children through an interpreter—a curious way to teach a language—beginning, not with a reading-book, not with a grammar, but with one of the very best specimens of French literature. His plan was to have them commit every word to memory. There it is—the first word "Calypso." He had them repeat it again and again after him until they knew it. He gave them a word at a time till they knew the whole sentence. Then he questioned them. The principle upon which he worked was that of learning one thing well, and comparing everything else with it. When he had taken up all of the first sentence—"Calypso could not console herself for the departure of Ulysses"—he asked questions. He had told them nothing about Calypso or Ulysses, except just what they could gain from that sentence. He asked them such questions as these: "Who was she?

What did she do?" He then took up the second sentence, and the third sentence, and, when they had learned all in this book, he turned them back and had them repeat it. After this we are told by M. Jacotot that those Dutch children used better French than he himself or any of the professors in the institution.

Mr. Joseph Payne, an eminent English teacher, took a boy eleven years old to teach him Greek. He wished to try experiments. The boy had been hammering away at the Greek grammar. Mr. Payne heard of Jacotot's method, and said he would try it with this boy. He did not use an elementary book, but began with the "Iliad," following the Frenchman's method, and when the boy had learned a few pages in this way he could read the whole. His testimony is that one can learn a language by this method in one tenth the time required by any other process.

With the word, the child learns to read. He repeats the word, giving all the different inflections. There is wonderful power in the human voice; it can express every emotion by means of the different inflections, rising or falling in pitch, and changing the tones, uttering words rapidly or slowly, with more or less force. This power can be shown by taking the letter "O" and giving in its utterance the various inflections of which the voice is capable. After the children get a few words, their vocabulary is rapidly enlarged.

CAUTIONS.

Primary reading is the important work. Everything depends upon a right start. There is too great a disposition on the part of inexperienced teachers to give long lessons at first, especially to small children. There is sometimes danger of giving to larger children lessons which are too simple. Here is an illustration of this: A gentleman teacher was exceedingly partial to some of Whittier's poems, and he had his class read "Maud Muller" day after day, week after week, and almost month after month. They would read it over and over again every day, and finally he asked if any one had a question to propound. One boy, who had been very patient, arose and said: "Professor, we have been talking about this fellow 'Maud Muller' for a long time. Now, I want to know who he was, where he came from, and what he was about."

There must be variety. A one-string violin makes poor music. The first words given to children should be short ones, and when a word is once learned well, there is no need of constantly repeating it.

For children of the first or lowest grade, three new words are enough to introduce at one lesson.

It is asserted by a good authority that, out of every ten hours devoted to reading in school, nine hours must be given by the pupil in trying to find out the author's meaning.

To read well, thoughtful study of the words, their meaning in combination or when standing alone, is an essential condition.

To enlist the pupil's attention, the lessons should be simple in character, interesting in matter, suited to the understanding, and elevating in their influence; and in every reader there should be some beautiful gems of literature, and these the children should commit to memory.

ADVANCED READING.

Instruction in the more advanced classes is somewhat different from that of the primary grades.

Not only must the pupil be able to pronounce the words correctly, but there is a wider scope for the exercise of all his mental powers.

In reading a paragraph, he must decide upon a combination of elements, and how each element is to be represented. The prominent ones are to be brought out in strong contrast with the weaker ones, the grouping preserved so as to bring into the mind of the hearer the harmonious blending which pleases the ear and satisfies the taste.

To read thus intelligently implies a critical and cultivated taste, and an ear and eye capable of appreciating the beautiful in thought and expression.

And while the voice may not be trained well enough to produce a pleasing effect upon the listener, yet the taste sets a higher standard than is reached, and the result is constant improvement in the delivery. The aim then of higher grade work in reading is to cultivate properly this critical faculty, and to set before the pupils each day higher conceptions of expression in utterance and action.

Since there is an intimate relation between the mind and the body, between thought and the thinker, between the thing as it is thought and the expression of the thought, the teacher never once loses sight of the fact that the body is the channel of communication between the two.

While the mind forms its conceptions, the body, as

the instrument of the mind, expresses to others the ideas thus formed. To give expression in a perfectly natural manner is what is meant " by studying nature."

As there is a language of the body, unwritten in the books, but known and understood by all men, the child should be trained that every movement of his body is the expression of a thought, and furthermore, that his work as a learner consists in perfecting himself so as to bring his bodily organism into complete subjection to his will. By utterance and action every style of thought—from the most tranquil to the most impassioned—can be expressed. When the pupil sits or stands erect; breathes naturally and can economize his breath; holds his book in the proper position; speaks the words with accuracy and precision, and in a pleasant and pure tone of voice, and is easily understood, his reading is such as any ordinary teacher may well be proud of; but to secure depth, volume, and elasticity of voice, daily practice upon the elementary sounds is absolutely necessary.

In summarizing the results to be accomplished by the pupil in reading, the following points are to be kept constantly in mind:

1. *To pronounce distinctly all the words so as to be heard.*
2. *To emphasize all the words so as to be understood.*
3. *To express the thought so as to be felt.*
4. *To attain clearness in expressing thought—separate and contrast ideas.*

Teaching Reading.

I. Object.
    1. Definition.
    2. To gain knowledge and pleasure.
    3. To give knowledge and pleasure.

II. Process.
    1. Talking.
    2. Seeing.
    3. Hearing.

III. Methods.
    1. Alphabet.
    2. Word.
    3. Sentence.
    4. Phonic.
    5. Parker's.
    6. Jacotot's.

IV. Elements.
    1. The intellectual element.
    2. The mental element.
    3. Vocal.
    4. Physical.

V. Talking.
    1. Object.
    2. Idea.
    3. Words.
    4. Association and reproduction.

VI. Seeing and Hearing.
    1. Object.
    2. Idea and word.
    3. Picture.
    4. Expression.

CHAPTER VIII.

TEACHING COMPOSITION AND LANGUAGE.

Composition is the art of expressing ideas and thoughts in words. It is of two kinds: oral composition and written composition. Written composition is divided into two kinds, also: ordinary school composition and higher composition. Of the latter there are many forms, the most common of which is that written for the press. This is seen in the newspapers and magazines, and presents every variety of subject of general, local, or temporary interest to the public. There are, besides this, historical, biographical, scientific, literary, and all the various forms which appear in books, and are of more general and permanent interest. I mention these departments because the work of the lower prepares for the higher.

I shall now speak particularly of that form of composition which pertains to common-school work.

Under the mental process, we have, first, to acquire knowledge; secondly, to elaborate or classify that knowledge; and, thirdly, to express it in language, either spoken or written. This is oral or spoken composition for which the children have made some preparation by talking, hearing, seeing, tasting, feeling, and smelling. They have made some acquisitions that we will call their own. In the school work the first object is to get the children to express their thoughts in language which is intelligible to other persons.

In the beginning the child learns how to talk from imitation, and from imitation alone. Observe the little child in his efforts to talk; he watches the movements of the lips, and imitates the sounds he hears. A person in learning a foreign language gets the peculiarities of pronunciation by imitating the teacher's voice. No book description can teach an American to pronounce the French language correctly. It is learned from the voice only. It has been said that few persons over thirteen can ever learn foreign languages so as to speak them without what is called an accent, so difficult is it to get the vocal organs into proper position to make new sounds after they have been employed for years in making certain familiar sounds.

It has even been asserted by some that a child learns to use a language almost exclusively by imitation, and should never study a grammar for that purpose; but that he should use it afterward for the purpose of determining whether a sentence is correctly or incorrectly expressed, and that this is the function of grammar. This opinion is worthy of serious consideration.

After the child has acquired the ability to talk, to express his thoughts in spoken words, comes this new acquisition, that of writing. It puts a new and greater power into a person's hands when he can, with the pen, write down his thoughts and send those written thoughts to others. It puts the thoughts into permanent form, preserving them for future or for distant use. In ordinary conversation we meet face to face to talk. Conversation is oral composition; but, having the ability to write, we can talk with persons on any other part of the globe.

Hence, one of the greatest discoveries made by man was that of the alphabet, giving him an easy means of communicating his thoughts to others. He puts letters together to form words, signs of ideas; and then these words together to form sentences, expressions of thought.

There are many methods of teaching the art of composition; attention is invited to a few of them.

Suppose we have a class of children, say six years of age, such as are found in the first or lowest grade. The teacher takes up some object, it may be a book; the children look at it; they talk about it. The teacher asks a few simple questions. It is not meant that a teacher is, or should be, an interrogation-point only, doing nothing but asking questions; but the teacher who can question skillfully, who knows how to draw out what there is in the mind of the child—a teacher who can use this, the Socratic, method properly—is always successful in his or her work.

As the children talk about the book, they become interested in it, and the teacher can write before the class on the board the word "book." Then ask the question, "Who can tell me something about the book?" Many hands go up, and some one, a little boy or a little girl, says, "It is a brown book," or "It is a large book." Let the children express themselves in short words, the teacher being careful to use words that the children understand. The teacher should then write the sentence on the board. If it is not expressed very well, have some one express it better, giving sentence number two. The question "Who will tell me something else about the book?" will bring up the little hands again, and some one is called upon to answer, and sentence number three is placed upon the board. Keeping on in this way, sentence follows sentence until there is a reading lesson. This method of teaching oral composition may be continued for a year or two, using familiar subjects.

After the children are sufficiently advanced, they may be questioned in regard to the object, and then, when they are able to do so, they should write on their slates, on the blackboard, or on paper, what they know of the subject presented, after proper directions have been given.

Another method sometimes pursued with fourth- and fifth grade pupils may be of interest. The teacher selects a list of words, say ten, and pronounces them to the school without telling the pupils how to spell them. They write the words as they think they should be spelled, and then look in their dictionaries for these words. This is a more advanced form of composition, and the children bring in the next day, or within the next two or three days, the ten words correctly spelled and defined. They don't know why these words were given, but on the second day the ten words are pronounced to the class as a spelling-lesson, and are spelled correctly. Then the teacher reads a short story in which these very words are used, and from which they had been selected without the name of the story being told to the children. The next day they reproduce the story as nearly as they can, putting into the sentences the ten words.

Another very good method of teaching composition writing in the intermediate grades is the selection of pictures by the teacher. The pictures are fastened on the wall of the school-room, and the pupils are asked to write descriptions of what they see in the pictures. The work is tested by comparing the composition with the picture.

Frequently very abstract as well as very dull subjects are assigned as suitable topics for school essays. A child can not call up much original knowledge "from the depths of his inner consciousness." The waters in that pool are usually turbid. The skillful teacher will avoid such topics.

Let the children write about things that they know, or something that they have done. Their own experience and observation should be woven into compositions. They may describe bits of travel, a visit, the school-room, and the articles it contains; a flower, an apple, etc. But the teacher should note how carefully and accurately the descriptions agree with the objects represented. For a child to describe well, he must observe carefully. A class of children had written very learnedly on "the cat"; but, when asked how many toes the cat has on its forefoot, silence reigned in that room. Yet these children had written on "hope," "rewards," "punishments," and "the elephant," prior to the exciting theme of "cat."

It is not intended to go into any elaborate account of methods of correcting compositions. Enough to say that, as penmanship is systematically taught in all grades of schools, there is no valid excuse for poor penmanship now unless some physical disability exists. Minute directions for marking all errors are given in most treatises on compositions, so that I have but few suggestions to offer.

1. The pupil should write a bold, legible hand.
2. He should display taste and judgment in the matter and form of his composition; that is, the manuscript should look as neat as possible in its general appearance, and impress the eye favorably.
3. Spacing, capitals, spelling, and punctuation must be rigorously attended to.
4. Small words are apt to be preferable to large ones.
5. Short, pointed sentences are better than long ones.
6. Write on one side of the paper.
7. In all cases of doubt, the pupil, if somewhat advanced, should consult the dictionary and English grammar.

The following expresses my views so fully that it is inserted at length:

"Not enough composition is taught in our common schools. To write a good composition requires time and hard work. Schiller, when he composed his poems, walked up and down the room repeating the verses to himself to see if they struck his ear well. The subject must not be too general; the subject must not be too difficult. The teacher should lend his assistance and instruct his pupils in the construction of correct sentences." *

"It is true that there is not enough composition taught in the common schools; it is equally true that there is not enough taught in the high-schools; in fact, there is very little *teaching* of the subject done anywhere. The work is required of the pupil, usually, and he is to 'make bricks without straw'; draw thoughts

---

* Professor Kemp.

from a brain that has no thought on the subject; express these thoughts in good language, when he has no command of language; arrange his topics in logical order, when he has no idea of either logic or order; and punctuate properly, when he has no knowledge of the utility of any mark save the interrogation-point. Composition, as it is usually taught (?) in the schools, is the bugbear of not only the pupil but the teacher. Instead of being daily work, like other studies, occupying the time which its great importance demands, it is a weekly work, usually, occupying perhaps an hour; instead of the subject being one that is within range of the grasp of the child's comprehension, it is one so far above his comprehension that he gropes in the dark hunting for some thoughts until the hour for writing is nearly closed, when he by accident stumbles upon something he thinks must be an idea, and, hastily grasping it, jots it down; instead of building up the work, from the single word to the simple sentence, from the simple sentence to the compound sentence, from the compound to the complex sentence, from the sentence to the paragraph, from the paragraph to the essay, they build downward, or try to, beginning with the essay, and, by the time the teacher has finished the corrections, ending with the word; instead of developing ideas of form, color, size, place, utility, difference, and agreement in their pupils, before they require them to write about objects that possess these qualities, these ideas are presupposed by the teacher to be already possessed by the pupil, with the power of arranging them in logical order. Imagination, observation, and concentration of thought are mental powers easily developed in the average child, and are inseparable requisites of good composition; yet it is true that, while they are easily developed in the average child, it is equally true that these powers exist as *possibilities* only in the young mind, awaiting either development or destruction. The average teacher requires a boy whose power of imagination has been all crushed out of him by the peculiar circumstances of his life to write a composition on a subject which requires the highest order of imagination; and thus with observation. Concentration of thought is required in all composition, yet pupils are required to write lengthy essays when this power has been so little cultivated that it might well be indicated by a term denoting less than zero. It is time that composition received the amount of consideration in all schools which its importance demands, and it is also time to revolutionize the work of teaching the subject, beginning at the bottom and teaching upward, instead of at the top and teaching downward." *

If the child is properly instructed, there is no reason why he should not write his thoughts with the same ease as he speaks them, and with more accuracy. This is possible only when writing his thoughts is a part of his daily school work. Constant and persistent practice of the right sort will enable the child to use the language as an instrument of thought. The habit of requiring pupils to copy their reading-lessons on their slates may become a positive hindrance rather than a help or aid to composition work. Pupils required to do a great deal of copying grow careless and work mechanically, and, in time, lose interest and put no thought-work into what they are doing. This may be tested in the following easy manner: Tell the pupils to close their readers, and then let the teacher read—only a few words at once—and ask the pupils to write what the teacher reads; to capitalize and punctuate the extract read. When the work is completed, ask the pupils to compare their work with the paragraph or paragraphs read by the teacher,

---

* Gertrude T. Johnson.

and which they copied. Note the variations from the text.

If it is a "new piece," the teacher should read it over once, slowly and distinctly; and then read it again a little at a time, for the pupils to copy. Compare results again.

The following directions should be kept in mind:

1. Let the little children write about things they have seen, things they have heard, or things they have done.

2. Let older pupils read over a lesson, close the book, and then reproduce it; lastly, compare their work with the original.

3. At dictation, require advanced pupils to write sentences of certain prescribed forms.

Illustration: To write a sentence having a *subject*, *transitive verb*, and an *object*, each of these elements modified by a *transitive clause*.

4. Give particular attention to the expression of the thought as well as to the thought itself.

5. Encourage the more advanced pupils to enlarge their vocabulary of words, and to discriminate sharply in the use of words.

6. In original composition: seek (1) a definite idea of what is to be said; (2) the choice of the right words to express it.

7. Aim at clearness in the expression of thought.

8. To acquire a graceful style, study the best writers.

Grammar.

Already the composition work involves a great deal of practical grammar. Grammar as an independent branch of study naturally divides itself into three departments, namely, the use of words, the relation of words, and the philosophy of words; and, if, instead of " words," we substitute " grammar" or "language," the analogy holds true also. Words are shadows of things, and all language instruction at first is to teach beginners how to use these shadows for the things themselves. Hence, practical grammar is that branch of the subject which enables the learner to use words correctly, and to judge somewhat of the thought expressed by the words employed.

As he advances in his school work, the parent or teacher begins to give him more positive directions in regard to the use of certain words—" articles," for instance—coupled with an injunction that "*you must*," or "*you must not*." This is only preparing the way for the higher form of work in the second division, when rules and positive reasons will be required and explained.

It is entirely proper and in accordance with actual experience that certain definitions should be taught to children as they progress in their studies. A child should know how to define a " *letter*, *syllable*, *word*, *spelling*, *sentence*," etc., by the time he is through the Third or Fourth Reader.

Good definitions, known and understood, enable pupil or teacher to stand alone and battle for himself.

Along with the kinds of sentences which the children early in school-life learn, the essential elements may be picked out, and even the parts of speech may be taught with some of their properties. Definitions should be generalized from examples.

In this connection, it is better to drop a suggestion in regard to "half-way definitions." Some years ago it was quite common to hear children speak of "telling sentences, asking sentences," etc. Of course, these descriptive terms are harmless, but sooner or later they have to be dropped by the pupils. In place of wasting time in learning or using them, teach definitions that need not be changed.

The sentence is the unit of thought, and it is with it that the philosophy of language begins. From the sentence the mind naturally passes to those elements or constituents composing the sentence, and then to the properties of these elements themselves.

Whatever classification is adopted by the teacher as to the form and the use of the sentence, it is also desirable that the "parts of speech," including their properties, relations, and uses, should be taught at the same time.

Technical grammar is studied for the express purpose of helping the pupil to use the language correctly, and to know why he uses one form of expression rather than another. This study enables the pupil to tell what the law of the language is, and, in its higher forms, *why it is*.

"Diagramming" a sentence is a method of symbolizing the logical structure of the sentence, and helps to bring out in a forcible manner its meaning. A particular diagram shows the meaning as interpreted by him who makes the diagram.

In the work of analysis, the following points should receive attention:

1. *The sentence as to its use.*

2. *The sentence as to its form.*
3. The essential elements.
4. The modifying elements.
5. The connecting and independent elements, if any.
6. The parts of speech, their properties, relations, and uses.
7. The reasons for the same.
8. Combine analysis, diagramming, and parsing.

Correcting exercises in " false syntax " is an excellent drill. For advanced classes, a thorough drill in some good text-book on grammar is absolutely necessary to sound scholarship and a critical knowledge of the laws and usages of our language. The agreements and differences of all the parts of speech should be thoroughly discussed.

THE THOUGHT ELEMENT.

Dr. Gregory found that a farmer's little son, aged six years, in one week used more than six hundred different words.

In the acquisition of our native tongue four different ends are to be attained, hence there are four different arts:

1. To hear and understand the spoken language.
2. To speak it.
3. To read and understand written or printed language.
4. To write it so that others may understand what is written.

The first two constitute spoken language; the other two, written language. The first two are acquired naturally, but the latter must be learned.

By a wise provision of nature the infant is an attentive listener, and becomes an interpreter of gestures and sounds before it can exercise its power of speech, being prompted through curiosity to observe all around it. As it grows older, all progress in spoken language is due to practice and imitation.

In the acquisition of a foreign language the process is somewhat different.

The order is the following:
1. The art of reading the language.
2. The art of hearing it.
3. The art of speaking it.
4. The art of writing it.

By the first two the words recall the ideas, and, in the second, the ideas recall the words. Lying at the foundation of all language culture are the trained eye, ear, lips, and hand: the eye to see, the ear to hear, the lips to speak, and the hand to write.

Intellectual progress is possible by noting agreements and differences. All knowledge may be arranged, according to Bain, under the following heads: persons, places, things, actions, results of actions, states or situations, and feelings.

Ideas first, the words that represent the ideas afterward, is Nature's method of teaching our mother-tongue. The sentence, which is a collection of words making a complete thought, is the unit of language.

How to express thoughts by words, either spoken or written, is the problem that the teacher is called upon to face in the school-room.

Every language-lesson should develop the thought-element by resolving the topic into its component parts, beginning at the first and presenting only one topic at a time, noting all its conditions and relations, and thoroughly mastering them before proceeding to the next difficulty. Strike in one place to make a "welding heat," is a safe adage in teaching.

The art of using language is acquired only by frequent and careful exercise. Attention to details is the condition to success. In every written exercise, on slate, blackboard, or paper, the following points are to be carefully noted by teacher and pupil:

1. The subject matter. 2. Neatness and the orderly arrangement of the parts. 3. Language and grammatical construction of the sentences. 4. Punctuation, spelling, and capital letters. 5. Penmanship.

To write or talk upon any given topic the writer must have some ideas in his mind that he can express in words, and consequently he must be familiar with some of the qualities or properties of what he proposes to describe. Its agreements and differences he has already observed. These acts, as simple as they may appear, involve all the elements of thought.

To set this in a still stronger light, suppose that a sentence is placed before the pupils for consideration. The sentence is a simple one: "The waves dashed high." What is in it? Evidently two ideas, "waves" and "dashed." If we stop at "waves," how suggestive the word! "Waves"—a thing classed under a form of knowledge; a part of a body of water; which is also a part of a larger body; which is a part of the great body, the ocean. Again, we may take another view of it and show its differences, which readily suggest themselves. But, next, the pupil's attention is called to the word "dashed," and he sets out finding agreements and differences, and how rich the results. Not content with the mere statement as a grammatical collection of words to be analyzed and then passed by, he goes further, and connects the ideas in this sentence with other knowledge that he already possesses. As to the mechanical execution, he looks out for capitals, punctuation, and penmanship. Further, he sees that the naked sentence contains two essential elements and two helping elements, and, by observation and induction, in due time he can formulate rules in regard to all the essential and helping elements in the English language.

To stimulate and direct the will-power of the pupil, and excite him to do the most for himself, is the best kind of instruction. To make him conscious of his own ability, and capable of using it successfully, is the primary work of the teacher. The pupil works, puts forth the effort spontaneously; the teacher seconds and directs his efforts. By degrees the learner, having confidence in himself, is prepared to study the language, not only in its relation to facts, but in its philosophy of facts. Thus, what is begun as an unconscious effort with the child, and acquired as a habit, may be developed into one of the grandest arts—the art of beautiful and elegant speech. For nice discrimination and the finer shades of meaning—the adjusting of words to the sense—certainly the structure of our language admits no superior.

To find *the word* implies the highest exercise of all the intellectual faculties, and in this respect language offers the whole range of science, art, and literature to select from. All languages then, for literary purposes, are living languages, and the only "dead language" is that "lifeless form" doled out to so many children in a parrot manner and labeled "grammar."

Composition.
1. Definition.
2. Mental processes.
    1. Acquiring knowledge.
    2. Elaboration.
    3. Expression.
3. Kinds.
    1. Oral.
    2. Written.
        1. Ordinary school.
        2. Higher forms.

Language.
1. Use of words.
2. Relations of words.
3. Philosophy of words.
4. Suggestions.

CHAPTER IX.

TEACHING PENMANSHIP.

"When he did sit down, he tucked up his sleeves, squared his elbows, and put his face close to the copy-book, and squinted horribly at the lines."—DICKENS, *Old Curiosity Shop.*

IT is not necessary to define writing; all know what it is; but, under this head of teaching penmanship, we must consider three things: First, what it includes; secondly, when to begin; thirdly, how to teach it. We have been accustomed to consider writing only in its mechanical aspects: skill in imitation and persistent practice were the only factors in producing a good penman. But the hand that does the work must be guided by the *will*, and before the will can exercise its function there must be in the mind a clear conception, a distinct picture of that which is to be reproduced.

Writing, as to its mechanical aspects, requires some preliminary conditions: First, position of the body, which should always be that least fatiguing to the person, and which gives perfect freedom to all the muscles of the arm and hand, and no part of its weight being permitted to rest upon the arm or table. The body should, therefore, be perfectly erect, whether sitting or standing at the desk, and the feet should rest squarely on the floor, particularly if sitting. Should you, reader, sit down to write, without placing your feet and limbs properly, you will discover that the body is at once thrown out of the erect position, and tends to follow feet and limbs into paths of crookedness. The head should be kept well up, not bowed as if in shame or grief, or seeking repose upon either shoulder. Resting securely upon its slender support—the neck—it can, by easy movements from side to side, save the eyes from strain as they follow the work in its progress on the page, always seeing every part of the line at the same angle, thus giving surer guidance to the hand, and securing a uniform slant to the letters. The arm should be at right angles to the lines across the page, and resting so lightly on the desk that it can move easily from side to side, carrying with it the hand that wields the pen. It is a notorious fact that very few pupils are found in any of the schools who take the proper position when they write. They seem so in love with the subject that they bend over to their work. It must be attractive, indeed, if the whole body must be distorted in the eagerness to "get down" to writing. Teachers should not fail to secure a strict observance of the requirements as to position, for upon this depends much of the success or failure in further instruction in penmanship.

In most city schools it has been for years the custom for pupils up to the middle of the third year to write on paper with lead-pencils. Having given much thought to the subject, I am now firmly of the opinion that pupils should begin writing with pen and ink in the lowest grade. Better results are secured, and pupils are pleased with it. The custom of doing so much writing with a lead-pencil is productive of careless habits, and consequently destructive of accurate and beautiful work with the pen in the hands of pupils, as the nice distinctions of curves and shading of which the pen is capable can not be made with a pencil. And then, again, pencil work is so easily soiled by handling as to make its use very objectionable in anything we may desire to preserve. Teachers object to the use of ink in the lowest grades because of inky fingers and spattered paper and desks. As this objection may be made to the first use of ink by pupils, let the grade be what it may, it strikes me that the neat habits necessary to its successful use would better be taught at the beginning of the course of study, and perpetuated by careful attention till permanently fixed, thus giving the teacher in the middle or upper grades less to do in habit forming, while the time can be more profitably spent in developing the thinking faculties.

Having insisted upon an easy position of the body, we come now to consider that of the hand which holds the pen, and how it holds it. But position is now to be combined with movement, and, as the conditions are more complex, more time and greater patience may be needed. Little feet totter when first they start out to tread life's pathway, and so little hands may not all at once come into or remain in a required position when in use. Do not discourage children by too rigid requirements at first. The pen-holding hobby is sometimes ridden to death. If teachers would talk less about holding the pen, and confine the attention of pupils more closely to the forms of the letters and movements necessary in making them, they would succeed better and with less labor, while nerves of both teachers and pupils would be spared much useless tension. As children's feet step more firmly after the practice which gives confidence to the mind, so will little hands gain skill and strength in time, and as the mind of the child under instruction becomes familiar with the forms of the letters, and eager to imitate a perfect copy, his hands adapt themselves to the requirements, and the pen-holding comes to take care of itself. This does not mean that the teacher should neglect this, but that he should not be impatient, and should take the child's hand gently in his own, quietly and tenderly guiding till it knows the way. Suppose they do fail at first; they try; encourage them. Very few teachers realize how weary grow the pupils' ears with the penholding din. A ball of yarn placed in the hand of a child with a challenge to see how long he can keep it there and yet scarcely touch it, has been found to aid materially in training the child's hand to take and retain the correct position. When a boy begins to use a knife—the joy of his early life, the companion of his riper years, and a precious memory when time has silvered his once dark locks and dimmed the lustrous eye—would you keep harping at him about holding it in a certain position? Boys and girls like to find out some things for themselves, and, in the matter of holding the pen, with very little guidance they will find out the best way. Persons who write a great deal tell us that they must frequently change the position of their hands, pens, and fingers, and that the position required by teachers is not always the best.

Here is a description of the method used by the Germans in teaching the position and movements of the hand and pen in forming the letters. When they begin lessons in writing, the letter to be imitated is first written so that the children can see it. Then the children describe the character, and imitate in air the movements used in making it. In this way they get a clear conception of its form and the necessary movements. Looking at it again, teacher and children together, at a given signal, describe it by movements in the air. This brings the muscles under control, so that the fingers are guided by the will. It is by working from that which is known and seen, connecting the movements with the mental picture, that the letter is easily and well made. This method gives practice in the full arm-movement, and control of all the muscles at the beginning, and the children soon learn to execute in a most rapid and beautiful manner.

After the preliminary instruction as to position and movements are understood by a child, he is to begin the work on paper, and it is very important that this introduction should be presented to him in a rational manner. I hold it to be true that writing is an intellectual rather than an imitative art, and that, as the sculptor has in his mind a definite conception of the form he expects to make from the block of marble, so must there be in the mind of the child a distinct picture of that which he is to produce on paper. Once made, he compares the production, the writing, with his mental picture, and criticises his own work. It is important that when a pupil looks at a letter he can tell whether it conforms to the model. Writing from this conception is not acquired by "writing," but from intelligent, critical practice. It is indeed possible for a child to practice so much that his writing shall grow worse and worse.

The steps in forming a letter are as follows: First, the pupil looks at a letter till he gets a clear conception of it; secondly, he tries to form the letter like the model placed before him; thirdly, he compares his work with the model, and notes the agreements and differences.

At first, the pupil should form the letters slowly, and always with care, writing more rapidly as he acquires skill in the use of the pen. The teacher should never allow him to acquire slovenly habits, but remember that eternal vigilance is the price of final success. In this branch of school work the result of poor teaching is seen more quickly than in almost any other.

The old plan of teaching writing was a very simple one, presenting the whole subject at once. The first lessons were in making straight lines and pot-hooks, and the only instruction regarding position was "Don't get your head too low"; and pupils were expected to write all the letters from the first. Now, the difficulties are mastered in detail. Requiring a pupil to write all the letters as his first exercise is like giving him the fifth reader on his first day at school. *It is the foolishness of teaching!*

The safer way is for the teacher to take one thing at a time. If there is no writing chart, the teacher, who should be able to write a good model, should place upon the board, before the class, a copy of the letter which is to be the lesson for the day. It is not necessary that the copy should be beautiful, but it should be perfect in form, and large in size. However, the teacher who can write beautifully can more easily interest children in the work, and get better results. Little folks have an eye for the beautiful, and will watch with eager interest while a teacher, skilled in the use of chalk or pen, leaves behind her moving hand well-formed and beautiful letters. They will improve even leisure moments in trying to " do likewise." While the above is true, it is quite possible for a teacher who can not write beautifully to teach well. I know one teacher who is a poor penman, but whose teaching power is so great that, without exception, her pupils write very beautifully. Her skill in getting pupils to do their own work so well is exceptional, but it shows that writing is not simply an imitative art, and that a teacher can, if she will, teach her pupils to do better work than she herself can do.

To those who maintain that writing is simply an imitative art, it may be asked, In what sense is it imitative? Can a human being imitate with his hand that which he can not perceive with some one of the senses, or of which he can not get a conception and form a mental picture? Does not the *will*, with action based upon this knowledge, direct the muscles? Does the hand act involuntarily when it imitates a form, a letter, a motion?

Again, if the attention of a writer is diverted for a moment, the hand goes astray, and the letter is a failure. Let any one try the experiment of giving attention to something else for a moment or two, and note the effect upon his writing. He could not claim that writing is not an expression of thought, or that it is possible to do two things well at the same time. As a further illustration of the importance of thinking about or teaching one thing at a time, let a beginner make the letter ℓ, and examine it. Can anything about it be pronounced perfect? No. What is the trouble? Too much has been undertaken at one time. He has not thought how each part should be made so that the whole letter may be correct. The first or upward stroke is not on the right slant; the second or downward stroke is a curved instead of a straight line, resulting in a poor, "bow-backed" affair. He had two ideas in his mind—one to reach the base line and the other to make the turn—when he made that downward stroke. The upward stroke was very nearly on the right slant, and he was all right on the downward stroke till a certain point was reached, and then all was wrong. The difficulty was mental. He thought of coming down and making the turn at the same time, and expressed the double idea that was in his mind; the idea not being clearly a unit, the expression was not clear, and therefore the letter is a failure, thus giving proof that it is very important to undertake but one thing at a time.

Suppose that a teacher gives to the child a whole letter. It is too much. Keep in mind the fact that a letter is made up of parts. The child can not make the whole letter correctly before he knows how to make each part composing it, or has at least in his mind a distinct picture of each part, and knows the order in which the parts occur. He must practice on that upward stroke till he knows it perfectly, then on the downward stroke, and finally on the finishing stroke. With a perfect conception of each part, and a knowledge of the movements by which they are made and united, he can, at will, make the whole letter. In this way the entire alphabet can soon be taught, taking one letter at a time. When a child is once thoroughly familiar with every letter in the alphabet, in its simple and its capital form, he can write words and sentences. Then, by practice, he becomes more and more perfect in the execution till he can write legibly, and perhaps beautifully.

It has long been a current theory that the best way to learn writing is to use a book with a printed copy, and keep the pupil imitating that copy. That is the way to learn *not* to write. The correct way to learn to write is to get a mental picture of each letter, a picture so perfect that it can be reproduced in the mind at any time. This form in the mind is an idea, and the written letter is the expression of this idea.

To recapitulate. The steps in making a letter are these: First, get a perfect mental picture; secondly, reproduce this mental picture; thirdly, execute, or make the letter. It is just as it is with an inventor: he has first in his mind the invention which he expects to give to the world; he invents it first, then expresses it in material form, visible to the eye.

The letter having been made, it is criticised by comparison with the model which is in the mind—the mental picture; or it may be criticised by comparison with a visible, material standard.

Penmanship is a *science* based on educational principles—principles just as fixed as are those of arithmetic—and the person who will study systematically till he forms in his mind a correct picture of every letter, and work to reproduce it, will learn to write well.

There is a method of tracing which is a process of mechanical imitation. There are copy-books that have thin leaves in them, and the child follows the form of the letter with the tissue-paper between the letter and the pencil. One objection, at least, may be made to this method. It takes up too much at once, and is not in accordance with the best of all educational maxims:

"One thing at a time, and that done well,
Is a very good rule, as many can tell."

There is one advantage in this method: the attention is easily concentrated by the device, and the hand becomes skillful in following the shading of the letters; but it seems to me that the same result can be best secured by training the pupil in the way already indicated, so that by a mental process he becomes capable, not only of doing good work, but of intelligently criticising his own work and the work of others.

Suppose, now, that a teacher wishes to train a class in penmanship—first, as a science, then in securing mechanical execution. The teacher takes a writing-book, and each pupil one similar to it. There is a perfect printed copy, and this copy a new letter—a letter they have not studied. At this new letter each one looks very carefully. The teacher questions in regard to the form of that letter, the parts composing it, the different proportions. They learn how to measure the letter, how to analyze it, how to compare their own efforts with the copy, and how to test the accuracy of their work. They can see their own mistakes, and describe in language the proper form of the letter. The whole class is sent to the board to write the letter "a," and "a" is written. Then they criticise, each his own work, and afterward each criticises the work of his classmates, telling in what the failures consist. In this way they are taught to criticise, and to express their criticisms in words. I am aware of the fact that in this detail work we must pass over many things. But it is systematic work. In writing, let each one do his best; let there be no careless work. Carelessness in writing must not be tolerated by the teacher, and all the written work connected with other lessons should be as carefully done as that of the special writing-lessons.

The objection with which we are met that system in writing destroys individuality is not valid. As well might we say that system in spelling, or in any other subject requiring the exercise of the thinking faculties, destroys individuality; and, since correct writing is the expression of distinct thought, and systematic thinking develops the individual mentally, we can not admit that a system of penmanship closely followed destroys individuality.

THE THOUGHT ELEMENT.

Penmanship is regarded by most persons as a kind of imitative art, consisting of ninety-nine per cent of practice, and perhaps one per cent of theory. The prevalence of this idea is the chief cause of so much illegible hand-writing among the educated classes, and in all seriousness some very intelligent instructors do not pretend that it should be taught in a systematic and logical manner.

Through the aid of writing-charts and copy-books the pupils of all schools may have excellent models for their guidance, provided the teacher has skill and tact in teaching the subject.

The best results I have ever seen in penmanship were achieved by two teachers whose hand-writing was very poor indeed; yet they taught all their pupils, without exception, to write legibly and beautifully. Their success depended upon their thorough knowledge of methods.

The true method of teaching penmanship is, that the correct form of the letter shall be studied till it is fixed as a reality in the mind, and then analyzed into its constituent elements, and each element practiced separately; and finally, by an act of synthesis, these parts united into one whole, or the letter. By this process a correct idea of the letter as a whole is obtained.

Following this is the next step, which is both mental and mechanical—mechanical in that the pupil attempts to put on the paper a faithful transcript of the form in the mind, or that he gives objective expression to his mental conception. But, should the intellectual act of the mind stop here, little progress is made, and penmanship degenerates into a dull, insipid drill. After the pupil makes an attempt to form a letter, he should know how to criticise his own work correctly. Hence, ability to criticise his own productions, using a correct ideal for a test, is the key to success in penmanship.

The following illustration will enforce this idea:

An ingenious writing-teacher has shown that, in the formation of the capital $\mathcal{O}$, twenty-four different things are to be observed:

First, left curve; secondly, straight line; thirdly, right curve; fourthly, oval turn; fifthly, left curve; sixthly, oval turn; seventhly, right curve; eighthly, loop; ninthly, right curve; tenthly, oval turn; eleventhly, left curve.

Measurement.

First, height of first stroke; secondly, width from same to left side; thirdly, full height; fourthly, top to junction with the first; fifthly, top to loop; sixthly, from first to second down strokes; seventhly, base line to last oval turn; eighthly, width of last oval turn; ninthly, from last stroke to loop.

Criticism of this Letter.

First, slant; secondly, angle of loop; thirdly, shading; fourthly, criticise the twenty points mentioned in the formation and measurements.

The same method of analysis holds of all the other letters—small and capitals.

The details of position—pen-holding, movement of the muscles—are a matter of practice; but the thought-element comes from first getting a correct picture or photograph of the letter in the mind long enough to put it down on paper. By means of this mental picture the pupil is his own critic, and in case of doubt he can appeal to the standard on the chart or to the writing-book.

Hence, penmanship as a science first appeals to thought, and secondly to the expression of thought, and in all cases the principles of this science should be taught from the very first day that the child enters school till he quits.

The following directions will assist the earnest teacher in doing this work well:

1. *That both feet rest firmly on the floor.*
2. *That the left hand rest firmly on the paper.*

3. *That the pen be held loosely in the right hand.*

4. *That the right arm and right hand be perfectly free in their movements.*

5. *That the nose, top of the pen-holder, and pen-point are in the same straight line with the main slant in the copy-book.*

6. *That the pupils be taught to criticise the size, slant, and space of each letter.*

The foregoing reflections and suggestions indicate in general the central thought that the branches should be taught so as to cultivate the "thinking faculties." Every branch may be so taught, but the branch is nothing in itself, the teacher is everything. "Who is the teacher?" is the important question.

WRITING.

I. What it includes.
    1. Mechanical execution.
        (*a*) Position, and (*b*) Movements.
            Body.   Head.   Hand.
            Feet.   Arm.   Pen.
    2. Intellectual.
        a. Mental pictures.   *e.* Synthesis.
        b. Reproduction.   *f.* Criticism.
        c. Expression.   *g.* Comparison.
        d. Analysis.

II. When to begin.
        a. With pen.
        b. With ink.
            In lowest grades.

III. How to teach.
        a. Show perfect model.   *e.* Criticism.
        b. Get mental picture.   *f.* One thing at a time.
        c. Reproduction.   *g.* Thoroughly.
        d. Execution.   *h.* Summary.

CHAPTER X.

TEACHING GEOGRAPHY.

SIMON TAPPERTIT, one of Mr. Dickens's characters, prided himself upon his ability "to eye things over." Primary geography is, pre-eminently, a study to be "eyed over," whether in nature or in a book. The words in the book tell about geography, while the real objects show what geography is.

Before the child is old enough to attend school, he has picked up considerable information on geography, but it is not assorted. By all means he should get his knowledge at first hand and from the best sources. The flowing river, the babbling brook, the pond in the meadow, the miniature island in the lake, the names of trees, birds, and flowers, are seen and learned by taking an afternoon stroll. What can be more enjoyable to little hearts than such a ramble? Pleasure and science both combined! How often such a lesson will reveal to the teacher dormant tendencies in children's characters that she never suspected of existing! Wherever there is a school-house, some objects of interest can always be found to illustrate many technical definitions in geography, if the teacher knows how to look for them and how to use them. As all knowledge is related to something that precedes it, and also to something that follows it, to carry out the law of harmony that subsists between what the child knows and what he does not know, he must begin with what he knows as so much capital stock and add each new acquisition to it. Should he commence with the unknown, the very remote, or obscure, and go to that which is still more obscure, bankruptcy is the inevitable result.

As soon as the child has become familiar with the real objects at home, those on the way to school, and those at the school-house, he is prepared to begin the process of representation, by making drawings or pictures, of the objects he has seen. This step is also accompanied with either an oral or written description of the object, thus uniting language instruction with geographical information. The latter process helps to fix the information in the mind.

At this stage in the learner's progress, many of his ideas are immature and need to be corrected by experience. Only in rare instances has he clear notions of distance, height, weight, size, and measure. Experience only can give this knowledge. Eventually, after repeated failures and mistakes, he is enabled to judge with a tolerable degree of accuracy. All progress comes through mistakes and corrections.

To draw a rude map of the school-house and surrounding objects is the first step on the way toward a definite conception of latitude and longitude, and the determination of a point on the earth's surface. The pupil must learn that location on a surface can not be fixed exactly except by the intersection of two lines crossing at right angles. It is not sufficient to fix the latitude—the longitude also must be ascertained.

When the child is sufficiently advanced to begin the primary geography as a text-book, the lessons should be read first in the class, the teacher questioning every pupil as to the meaning of each topic. Judicious questioning should bring to the surface what the pupils think the meaning is, rather than the teacher's views. The skillful teacher draws out adroitly the pupils' information, and corrects mistakes afterward. By the time the pupil begins the primary text-book, he ought to be able to multiply and divide numbers, and consequently to estimate distances on the maps, and to convert by the "scale of miles" map-measurements into statute miles.

The sand and molding-board hobbies are base deceptions that can not be employed by persons "who have a *very* sacred regard for truth." Any ordinary molding-board product must of necessity be so overdone as to convey the grossest exaggeration, a thing certainly to be avoided in teaching children conceptions of real things. Not long since the writer had occasion to examine one of the molded maps of the United States.

Comparing the depression of the Mississippi River with the elevation of the Appalachian Mountains on the east and the Rocky Mountains on the west, the channel of the river was about five hundred miles below the two mountain systems. Certainly the teacher is intrepid who would teach children relations between natural objects so far from the truth.

In primary geography, the book should be used chiefly as a reader, and not as a work to be committed to memory and to be recited *verbatim*.

As far as possible the pupils should illustrate the meaning of each paragraph from their own experience. After the lesson is read and understood, the pupils may close their books and answer the questions connected directly or remotely with the subjects mentioned in the lesson.

The intelligent teacher will not take the words that the pupil uses for a complete expression of the thought he has in his mind. At this stage of the learner's progress, he is busy in trying to get ideas out of the books he reads, and particularly so when the book he reads is geography. In this study, as in most others, the pupil must depend largely upon faith. He is obliged to take for granted what others say. His eyes can take in only a very limited portion of the earth's surface. Hence a few definitions, a little observation of his own, and a large mass of information gained from the records and observations of others, will constitute his geographical information, even should he make great progress in this interesting branch of science.

Advanced Geography.

Leaving what is called primary geography, the pupil is prepared to take up, under the title of "Advanced Geography," some of the most interesting topics of study connected with our earth, such as its position, shape, size, density, physical features, etc., as compared with other bodies in the same system. Ritter tells us how the three great natural kingdoms, mineral, vegetable, and animal, though each having an independent form, are related in a three-fold way to the earth's surface and to human history.

Viewed in this light, geography becomes an intensely interesting study, as leading all the way from nature's lowest forms to God, whose breath gave spirit to his image—man.

The whole surface of the globe is condensed into an epitome on a mountain side; yet we hardly realize it. All the changes that a few miles of travel from the level of the ocean to the top of the mountain can give are such as a person would experience in traveling for weeks or months from the burning regions of the torrid zone to the perpetual cold of the frigid.

In the study of geography we are brought face to face with those grand manifestations of physical nature which fill our hearts with awe and reverence. Here it is that the thoughtful student catches glimpses of those mysterious currents of air that circle the earth from pole to pole, and those still more majestic rivers in the ocean, whose banks never overflow; and yet these themes, so captivating, receive little or no attention in most schools, while memorizing names of unimportant objects occupies nearly all the learner's time. It is true that local geography, or geography of *place*, may be learned by committing detached names, provided the learner is favored with a retentive memory; but it is a more rational method for the learner, when reading history or the newspaper, and finding references to localities on the earth's surface, to provide himself with a map for reference, so that he can locate those places about which he reads. Suppose it be the "Retreat of the Ten Thousand": with the map spread open before him, the reader traces out the marches and countermarches of Xenophon and his heroes. He learns to know the people and the general characteristics of the country which they traversed.

To understand Napoleon's campaigns, his retreat from Moscow for instance, what can make a more vivid impression upon the mind of the reader than to follow day by day that famishing army through the snows of a Russian winter? To appreciate the perils experienced in the Arctic regions, take the map, and as you read follow the weary footsteps of the explorers. To know even the history of our own country during the dark and gloomy period of the Revolution, the paths of the contending forces must be followed from day to day.

Let the learner begin with a blank map, which contains the parallels and meridians and the coast-lines. As he reads, he locates places, rivers, mountains, etc., and, by the time he is through the book or subject, he will have acquired a good geographical knowledge of the country. The map grows daily under his own eye and hand. He literally knows it, for he has made it.

Thus time and place are both associated, and Geography and History join hands not to be divorced. They are dependent upon each other. In their union the seeker after truth is led out of the mechanical details of the subject and endows it with a higher life. The dry bones rattle no more, and, instead of a task for dull minds, there is a theme of fascinating interest and surprising beauties.

Geography is the science that opens the gateway to the other great departments of organic and inorganic nature. On the one hand is spread out in the grandest profusion the whole vegetable kingdom, with its myriad forms, whether growing on the earth or in the sea; one step more, and the rocky leaves of the book of nature are turned, and the history of the animal kingdom is read in the silent but emphatic language of the past, telling of the eras before man, the highest type. The earth was made for man, and geography tells us the story of its preparation. Shall we not cease to teach geography, then, as a collection of isolated facts? Let us unite these facts into one grand truth. Then we shall rise above the level of lifeless form into the region of the spiritual—from the created to the Creator.

It is interesting to study about the plants and animals which vary with the altitude as with the latitude. Geography leads us into the great field of botany, and from that to the animal kingdom, with its extinct species imbedded in the bosom of the earth, telling us of its changes before even man, who came last and highest, began his dominion over all the earth.

More important still are the social and intellectual conditions of men, and those peculiarities which distinguish one nationality from another. Historians for a long time wrote of the rulers, and but little was said about the people. Now, men are studying into the social and intellectual conditions of the people themselves; they wish to know why some nations have risen to the plane they now occupy; why all this culture; why the schools, the press, the railroad, the steam-engine, and everything that tends to make man better, happier, wiser. These questions are springing up in the minds of thinking men and women everywhere; and I know of no class of persons more capable of investigating these subjects than teachers. They should be well versed in social science, in political economy, and in all kindred topics. Not only should they be able to answer the questions children ask, but they should be able to answer the questions of the age.

Mighty issues are coming forward for solution in all civilized countries. The intelligent teachers will help in the work of conducting the nations safely through these stormy periods. Knowing clearly the natural and acquired rights of the citizen as a member of the state, they will prepare the school children to assert their personal rights and to perform their duty to the state. A clear understanding of social and political duties, and of the complex relations between the various industries and occupations, all teachers should possess. No longer can the teacher be a mere "school-master." He must be a citizen of the world, and he must stand and feel where its great heart beats the strongest.

Religions, beliefs that men have, have always attracted more attention than anything else. They are beliefs in the unseen, and all have them. Comparing these beliefs, we learn to be tolerant. All truth is not with us. Truth is many sided, and different persons look at it from different points, no two seeing it alike, though one person may be just as conscientious as another person.

Hence it is that the geography of nature leads us to the geography of man, and opens up to us the grandest themes which can be presented to the human mind for contemplation. All the earth was made for man, and there is not one interest of his, from the lowest animal want to the highest spiritual longing, that is not provided for; and geography tells us the story of that provision.

NATURAL SCIENCE.

Reaction is strong against the usual methods of teaching natural science in all grades of schools and colleges, and to-day the question is, Shall we use the synthetic or the analytic method, or combine them, in teaching science?

Common sense answers by saying, "Use both." The beginnings of the natural sciences are founded upon the observation of facts which, with their phenomena, are arranged, classified, reduced to systems according to the laws which produced them. To account for the present existence of things and phenomena is the province of the natural sciences.

God's will is the natural law, and man is the interpreter, and the correct interpretation depends upon man's ability to read the volume of nature as it is written. This brings us to the question of how to study and how to interpret nature.

Formerly, nature was studied too much in the closet; the whole system of the universe was elaborated from lamp-smoke and bad air. But it is the present conviction that, to get definite knowledge, objects themselves must be examined, and the knowledge had at first hand.

Before the child goes to school, considerable scientific knowledge has been acquired, not only of the land and water, but of animals, vegetables, and in some instances of minerals. This knowledge, it is true, is in fragments, but the teacher can assist the child in grouping it into classes.

Undoubtedly the child should begin the study of all the natural sciences in the objective form first; and not from definitions in books, or from pictures, or maps. The true order is the object, the word next, or the expression of the idea represented or aroused by the object; and lastly, the picture or representation of the object. To begin with definitions is to put the general notion before the individual idea—a reversal of nature's method and of the experience of the race.

To illustrate the above: Geography, a subject studied in all our common schools, is most frequently taught from verbal definitions and map-drawing. But before the pupil goes to school he possesses quite a fund of detached information on this subject, and he should begin with what he knows, and proceed from the known to the unknown.

Again, the true idea of the map having been taught, the pupil should find out how to measure distances, using the "scale of miles" and ruler for this purpose. Other relations will also be ascertained which will greatly aid the pupil in getting a proper estimate of distance and direction. Immediately following this is attention to parallels and meridians. To appreciate this means of fixing location, it should be borne in mind that all points on planes are located by the intersection of two lines, and that distances are measured from their intersection. This simple idea is the central thought in all astronomical and terrestrial computations pertaining to distances and areas, and is the natural key to map-drawing.

Early in the study of geography the pupil should be encouraged to classify his knowledge and to systematize it. Too often it is learned and recited in "broken doses." For instance, any particular country when studied by advanced pupils may be outlined under the following divisions: 1. Position. 2. Physical features. 3. Natural productions. 4. The inhabitants. 5. Their improvements. 6. Their institutions. 7. Differences from other countries as well as similarities. These topics should be expanded by the pupil and the subdivisions filled.

Rising still higher is the department of physical geography, which is the philosophy of our earth and all that pertains to it.

In its relations to other bodies it is a planet, composed of land and water, surrounded by an atmosphere. In its history it reveals the past through its dead forms, and its present life by its living ones. Not only facts, but the philosophy of facts, tempt us into one of the most inviting fields of nature.

Pouring knowledge into passive minds is erroneous teaching. Gathering knowledge by the mind itself is true instruction. Teachers should only stimulate the pupil to independent work. Let it be remembered that none of the natural sciences are to be studied from books alone. Books are only helps—not masters—and teachers and pupils should not be slaves to them. From direct contact with facts, the pupil must draw his conclusions by memorizing less and thinking more. With each pupil two objects are sought to be accomplished, namely, habits of mind, and methods of thinking.

GEOGRAPHY.

Primary.
    1. Home.
    2. School-house.
    3. Village, town, etc.
    4. County.
    5. State.
    6. Nation.
    7. Continent.

    1. Situation.
    2. Boundary.
    3. Sketch; Map.
    4. Surface.
    5. Climate.
    6. Waters.
    7. People.

Advanced.
    Nature—Earth.
        1. Position.
        2. Shape.
        3. Size.
        4. Relief.

        5. Climate.
        6. Vegetation.
        7. Animals.

    Man.
        1. Races.
            Primary.   Secondary.
        2. Organizations.
            Social.   Civil.   Religious.
        3. Governments.
        4. Industries.

CHAPTER XI.

TEACHING HISTORY.

Four questions present themselves upon the threshold of this subject:

I. *Why Teach History?*
II. *When Teach It?*
III. *How Teach It?*
IV. *What Effect should be Produced?*

These topics will be discussed in the order they are numbered.

I. Why Teach History?

As soon as the child begins to reflect upon his own existence and surroundings, he connects himself in some way with those about him. He hears his parents speak of relatives and friends, and he is aroused to the fact that he is related to his parents' relatives. Their friends and acquaintances also are not so far removed from him as entire strangers. Gradually his field of experience enlarges, and he begins to trace backward, by questioning, the history of individuals and other objects. This desire to find out the origin of things is instinctive with the race, and is, when exercised in the direction of history, only one of the many indications of the normal action of the mind.

All knowledge is first individual experience. Each individual is therefore constantly enlarging his circle of knowledge by his own observation and the testimony of others. It is certainly natural for the child to be inquisitive in regard to those things that concern himself and those with whom he is acquainted.

In this sense, then, the child commences the study of history—that is, personal history—long before he enters the school-room. Even here he still continues the process of gathering facts and arranging them, oftentimes crudely enough, into a dim historical whole. With this indistinct outline, the child enters school. His surroundings are different from those of home. He is thrown into a busy, organized community of which he is a member. Right and justice stand side by side with him now. Certain things he must do and others he must avoid. Adjusting himself to his new surroundings, the idea of obedience to authority, because it is commanded, is forcibly inculcated. Back of the school authority he learns soon to discern other powers manifested in the presence of civil officers. Thus is he introduced to the state, and made to feel that he, too, is in some sense an object of interest to this higher power.

But in this country, where the ballot of one individual may elect the chief magistrate to the highest office known to our laws, the *history of the country* is an essential branch of a common-school education. Intelligent citizenship is the primary object of studying history in the common schools. This demand is a requirement of the age. It is imperative and must be obeyed. Our civil, political, military, religious, and social institutions are different from those of all other civilized nations of the globe. The idea that our career has thus far reached in history is: that of universal education and absolute equality of all citizens before the law.

The plea that I now make is: that all our children should become more thoroughly imbued with the spirit and genius of our institutions; that our national history, with all its struggles for freedom, is as much of an inheritance for the child whose eyes first opened on the other side of the Atlantic as it is for the one born in our own native land. In no other way can we counteract those wild and vague notions so foreign to our institutions and so detrimental to our peace and prosperity.

It has been truthfully said that the permanency of our government depends upon the intelligence, the virtue, the wisdom, and the patriotism of our citizens. Patriotism is innate in the human breast, but parents and teachers should direct it aright.

The little boy of to-day is the voter of to-morrow. With these obligations resting upon him, he should come to the ballot with a clear understanding of what it means and what it represents. Back of the ballot should be seen freedom, purity, and patriotism; one country, one hope, one destiny—and that universal progress. *Burn it into the hearts of our children that the destiny of America is the destiny of humanity!*

II. WHEN TEACH IT?

Under this division, the following subdivisions naturally arise:

1. Facts.　2. The relation of facts.　3. The philosophy of facts.

These subdivisions correspond somewhat to the

order in which the human mind is developed. If this classification is founded upon a correct interpretation of mental development, then the teacher's work is greatly simplified, and the question relates to the predominating stage of mental activity, and the kind of knowledge appropriate to that stage. At this point no mistake should be made. Two topics here must be considered, the order of development, and what kind of knowledge is required to produce the necessary result; or, more specifically, what kind of history is appropriate at any stage of the learner's progress?

1. The history of our own country is of first importance to the American boy or girl. Let us suppose a class of pupils able to read fairly well in the Third Reader. What should such a class read? I reply: Some good work containing stories of American history. No school-boy can read such a work without kindling his patriotism over the story of the trials, the struggles, and the self-sacrificing devotion of our forefathers to those principles of freedom for which they risked their lives and fortunes. Such stories, if told in simple yet touching language, go home to the heart. The child can not read them unmoved.

2. Coming one step higher, we meet the admirable primary histories issued by our enterprising publishers. While they treat chiefly of facts, yet the relation of facts is brought somewhat into view.

These books are intended for Third and Fourth Reader pupils, and should be used as supplementary readers. It should be remembered that a majority of school-children never go beyond the Fourth Reader, and they ought to get some knowledge at least of our national history before leaving school. A taste formed for historical reading thus early in life will grow and strengthen with the years as they glide by.

Perhaps the most important event in the little child's life is the reading of his *first book,* not his school-reader, but some volume that he takes up and reads through and through. How he goes back and pores over again and again the most interesting pages and makes them his own, how he returns to them in after years, and how unaccountably he lingers there and drinks from the fountain that quickened and slaked his thirst in the bright sunshine of his youth! It is true that the first book may not have been one of great merit, yet on the clean, unscratched tablet of the memory it stamped impressions deep and lasting. They were the first, and they are always fresh and living. Where is the American boy that read in early life Weems's "Life of Marion" without receiving such an impression? It paints a character pure and lofty, and moved always by the noblest impulses of a dignified and generous nature.

The life lessons there so strikingly portrayed are such as every boy should learn. But this is only one book among many that may be placed in the hands of children helpful in the formation of character.

3. At this stage the pupil is able to take a higher view of men in action. Time and place are accidents in the unfolding of irresistible forces, which man may partially direct, but is unable to control. Before his mind a moving panorama is placed, and nations come and go on the waves of time. The birth, the growth, maturity, decline, and decay, are written of those that once were, but now are not. He studies each for a predominating

idea—the national characteristic. This central thought embodies the philosophy of the nation's existence. It is compared with the central ideas of other nations, and the agreements and differences are noted.

To the student of history, be he statesman, philosopher, or teacher, the philosophy of history is one of the grandest themes. It goes to the most exalted heights and descends to the lowest depths. In verity it is the bond that unites many factors into one complex whole.

III. How Teach It?

The fact that history is so unpopular is owing to the manner in which it is taught. All the soul is taken out of it. A few disjointed, ill-shapen facts are strung together and called "history," and repeating these verbatim is called a "history recitation."

There are two principal avenues to the mind—the eye and the ear; and, in teaching, both are to be employed. History, then, must be presented objectively to the eye: its leading facts grouped and spread before the eye of the pupil, on chart, paper, or blackboard, and dwelt upon till they become a part of the mind's furniture. Through the eye the understanding is reached most effectively, and, besides, the habit of classification, one of the chief benefits derived from the pursuit of any branch, is stimulated to a healthy activity in the arrangement of facts, their causes and sequences. To facilitate the teaching of history, charts have been prepared, showing at a glance the leading events of any period and their locality. The nations are represented by different colors, so as to trace their history with less difficulty. By referring to the chart, a moment only is necessary to determine whether at a certain date a nation was progressing or receding in political importance.

The lesson assigned must be definite in extent, commencing at a certain paragraph and closing with as much precision, and with additional instruction to aid the class to find out whatever is available from other sources on the subject. This is beneficial in stimulating to new fields of thought. The lesson being prepared, the class is called by signals to the board. For convenience, the class may be divided into three or more sections, and numbered as sections 1, 2, 3, etc. Section 1 may draw a map of the country and indicate the localities mentioned in the lesson; section 2 may write exhaustive analyses of the lesson on the board; members of section 3 may prepare condensed reviews of previous lessons. Besides the work mentioned, a large blank map can be used to great advantage in this manner: Draw a simple outline map of the country, and, as the class advances, one or two members can fill in the details day by day. The map grows with the progress of the class. Colored crayon is recommended in drawing this map. Two fifths of the recitation can be devoted profitably to this written work, and the work should so alternate that no pupil does the same kind of written work during two successive recitations. Every member of the class must work, and it is the teacher's duty to see that this requirement is strictly complied with.

During the remaining portion of the recitation, the work should be oral. *Undivided attention* is the first condition of a good recitation. Each member of the class should be held personally responsible to commence or to continue a topic whenever called upon by the teacher. Pupils are to use their own language, express their thoughts in pleasant and agreeable tones of voice, and speak the language correctly. Boys frequently say what they do not intend, and stammer and hesitate for words. To remedy this defect, they should be permitted to try till they tell all there is to be said. The common practice of excusing from further recitation as soon as a mistake is made can not be too severely censured. Here, two extremes are to be avoided: the first, too much talk on the part of the teacher; the second, permitting a few good pupils to do the reciting for the class. A proper distribution of work is indispensable in the school-room. Corrections in spelling, capitals, punctuation, pronunciation, language, and the material facts of the lesson, ought to be made by the class. A healthy spirit of criticism is a powerful incentive to correct scholarship and accuracy in every respect.

With respect to grouping important events in general history, a few words may not be devoid of interest.

As an example, the sixteenth century is chosen. It is pre-eminently a century of storms—political, ecclesiastical, and intellectual. They burst in tornado violence on the nations of Europe, uprooting and overturning old institutions.

France, England, Spain and Germany stood confronting one another. Early in the century, three young monarchs had ascended the thrones: Francis I, of France, Henry VIII, of England, and Charles V, King of Spain and Emperor of Germany. Each was bold, daring, unscrupulous, and ambitious. The discoveries made in the new world had aroused the minds of the people to independent inquiry and bold investigation.

During this period, Luther's pen and voice shocked, then stirred to action, the religious world. The contest was soon transferred to the battle-field. Never before in the world's history had the human mind asserted its spiritual freedom.

From this starting-point, the student may trace the current of history backward into the ignorance and gloom of the dark ages, or go forward, keeping pace with the tide of civilization. It is unnecessary to multiply illustrations; the teacher can select them.

IV. What Effect should be Produced?

Hitherto the pupil is supposed to follow the current of history without entering fully into the spirit of it, only in so far as he comprehends the motives of the actors themselves. He has arrived at that critical stage in his mental development when he is partially prepared, at least, to enter wider spheres of human activity, and to contemplate the actions of men as the resultant of forces designed to accomplish specific purposes. He so far forgets himself for the time being as to become Greek, Roman, Crusader; in short, he thinks, lives, and feels what he reads. As the nations come and go upon the ever-changing scenes of time, he follows their entrances and exits, and learns from their birth, progress, maturity, and decay, that they, too, are governed by universal laws. From all these lessons of the past he accumulates knowledge which enables him to compare the civil, political, military, and religious institutions of the ancients and moderns with those of his own country. Having his mind well stored with such information, he is better qualified to discuss all public questions, of whatever nature, than the one who is unable to draw practical lessons from the experiences of other nations.

Should the student take our country as his model, he must know its history in all its minutiæ as well as in its boldest outlines, and then compare the history of other countries with it, and note the differences and agreements as he prosecutes his inquiries. Material gathered, classified—conclusions deduced—are the steps in the mental process. There was a Greek civilization different from ours, yet ours is flavored with Athenian thought; a Roman civilization certainly not ours, but we have borrowed much from it; from the forests of Germany, the sunny plains of Italy, the valleys of France, the lowlands of Holland, the hills of Scotland, and the downs of England—each and all have contributed elements to our civilization. To pick them out and assort them is the task of the special historian; yet, after this refining process is carried out to the last analysis, there will be found much that is distinctively American. Climate, circumstances, laws, manners, customs, distinctive traits of character, even wit and humor, cause one nation to differ from others.

In our country man is the unit, and his individuality is offered the fullest and freest scope. No barriers are imposed to arrest his highest forms of mental, moral, and social development. Authority and liberty join hands, and the freedom of the individual is limited only by the welfare of the whole.

As a mere matter of fact, it is not very important to know that Columbus sailed from a port in Spain on the 3d day of August; but it is important that he sailed, discovered an unknown world, and that it was colonized by the best blood of Spain, and that, while Spaniards settled the new world, Spain lost her supremacy in the old world.

To comprehend the differences existing between our laws, manners, customs, modes of education, commercial, manufacturing, and agricultural pursuits, and those of other nations, the pupil is obliged to familiarize himself with the fundamental principles upon which governments are instituted, laws are enacted and carried into effect, and the rights of individuals and the liberties of the people are secured. Society, under whatever aspect it is viewed, is a complex organism, and governmental authority in different countries is maintained and exercised under widely different forms. To compare these forms and to study them; to ascertain how the civil, municipal, and other authorities settle disputes and administer justice among men, are subjects of the greatest importance in the education of the citizen who is to prize the form of government under which he lives.

Not only should the intelligent citizen clearly understand the origin, development, and nature of our government, with its marked outlines and co-ordinate departments nicely and wisely adapted to one another, constituting a compact system that rests for its support upon the affections and reverence of the people, but he must also understand how it is, as an expression of the popular will expressed by representatives on the one side and the consent of the people on the other, opposed to those forms of government whose citizens have had no hand in forming and no voice in approving.

That a citizen in some sense has had a hand in shaping the form of government under which he lives, and that he has compared his own workmanship with that of other people, and that it does not suffer in the comparison, tend to beget a contentment with the present condition of affairs, and a disposition to prevent radical changes in politics without due deliberation. If evils exist, he prefers peaceable means at the ballot-box as a corrective. Confidence in the people exists, and he knows that the people get close enough to the fountain-head to make and to unmake congressmen, senators, and presidents. This is the ever-present remedy he relies upon for changing the existing order of things. Upon every hand is felt the strong power of the government, manifested more in its moral influence than in its official capacity. Everywhere civil officers abound, but, excepting policemen, without the insignia of office. Should his knowledge by travel be enlarged, he is impressed upon every hand by the continual presence of national officials, tax-gatherers, civil magistrates, and other public functionaries.

Experience has taught the pupil somewhat of the duties of the various township, county, town, city, state, and national officers, how they are elected or appointed, and he naturally inquires what duties corresponding officers in other countries perform, how they are appointed, and the limits of their functions. Such inquiries open up a boundless, though not a useless, field for investigation. It will show that the roots of our civil system lie deep in the nations that preceded ours, and that, in a large degree, our form of government is eclectic. Under all climes human nature is pretty much the same, and man is never degraded in using power except when he consciously and willfully abuses the authority entrusted to his keeping.

History as such must always be read in the light of motives. If the student of history interprets it by any other light, he is journeying across an unknown sea without chart and compass.

To teachers of history I can not conclude this topic in a more becoming manner than by quoting the following extract:

"We educate the future citizens of the United States, not the future citizens of Prussia, of France, of England, of China, or of Japan. This must dictate our methods. Nor shall we forget that, although citizens of the United States, they are to be men and women. The particular shall not swallow up the general: We will not educate Spartans. Nor shall the general obliterate the particular: We will not educate blank abstract humanitarians."

CHAPTER XII.

TEACHING ARITHMETIC.

Mr. Darwin tells us that, when three persons went into a thicket in which a magpie had its nest, it would fly away, and wait for the three to go out before it came back; but that, when more than three went into the thicket together, and then went out one at a time, it became confused; clearly indicating, as he thought, and as many believe, that the bird could count up to that number, three, and retain it in its mind; but that above three it was unable to keep a correct record. There are some persons, and it may be said some tribes of people, who appear to be unable to count to any extended degree. Beyond five, ten, or twenty, they can only represent the numbers which they can not comprehend. The idea of number is evidently intuitive, and the disposition to count seems to have its origin in the distribution and collection, the separating and the bringing together, of things used in the common transactions of life. This gives us the basis of all mathematical reasoning. Arithmetic has, from the time of the ancient Greeks, been regarded as one of the essential branches of study in school. Should you ask today what two studies are most important in our school-work, the reply would be, without hesitation, "reading and arithmetic," because upon these two depend all classification in the lower grades of schools. Reading is the *key* that unlocks the door of the temple of knowledge; and, if we consider it in the sense in which the Germans use it in their schools, it includes grammar, literature — everything that we bring under the term "language." It is by means of language that we communicate and receive knowledge on all subjects, and hence it is the "key."

Arithmetic is the basis of all classification of pupils. In putting this subject prominently forward, I would not be understood as underestimating in any degree the importance of other branches.

Two objects must be kept in view in teaching arithmetic: first, accuracy; secondly, rapidity; but these are the results of attentive practice. Above these, however, is the development of the faculty of consecutive thought. Arithmetic is to most children a pleasing study. They love certainty in their work; and this study, properly taught, carries with it that degree of freedom from error which places it upon a higher vantage-ground than can be accorded to the other common branches. Yet, as it is usually presented in the textbooks, it is dry, and requires the greatest tact and skill upon the part of teachers to make it attractive and interesting.

Many methods have been proposed for teaching arithmetic to small children. It is not our purpose, nor would it be appropriate, to pass judgment upon them now. There is something good in every method. But the average child knows more than the teacher gives him credit for, and the routine drill which is too commonly practiced, and which ignores what the child already knows, stupefies instead of stimulates the intellectual faculties.

The human mind delights to see truths under a variety of forms, and to reduce new and complete forms back to original and known elements. This is why a devotee of mathematics finds such exquisite delight in unraveling intricate relations and expressing them in known symbols.

The trouble which so many teachers experience in getting pupils to understand arithmetic is not inherent in the subject itself, nor in the mental inability of pupils to comprehend it, except in rare instances, but is owing entirely to defective methods of instruction.

Not many years since an assistant superintendent of schools in a Western city concluded that the pupils there could not learn arithmetic because of certain atmospheric conditions which, in some mysterious manner, obscured the mathematical faculty. The reason for this defect was not in the atmosphere, unless in that of the schoolroom. Haziness probably existed in the mental atmosphere of the teacher.

When a mother says to me that her daughter can not learn arithmetic, I feel sorry for both mother and daughter, though not satisfied that her statement is correct. There may be imbeciles, unable to learn arithmetic or any other subject, and there may be those who make slow progress, but the difficulty is usually owing to the fact that the subject has not been properly presented. Some pupils learn more easily than others, but it is quite certain that the ordinary rules of arithmetic can be learned by any person not an imbecile.

The most difficult part of this problem is in teaching arithmetic to beginners. The mind of the child ought to expand gradually in all directions, and should not be confined in its actions to mere mechanical drill, lest it lose its elasticity and buoyancy. Pupils commence arithmetic as soon as they enter school, and it is at the beginning that most care is to be exercised in avoiding that air of abstractness which is made to surround and mystify a subject that would otherwise be easily understood. No number should be given them without its application to objects which they can see. Let it be to them clearly a concrete number.

Suppose we visit a school-room together in which there are seventy pupils about six years of age. There is a nicely carpeted platform for the teacher, and on this platform a table with a beautiful cover on it. In the room is a large number of pictures—some hanging on the walls, others resting against them. On the table are more than fifty different kinds of objects that the eye can see: rubber dolls, several of one kind; 'little pewter pans; little shells, that have been picked up by the children; and many other little objects. Note the character of the exercises. The children have been in school but a short time. At first, they were liable to forget where their seats were, and lose themselves; but now they will, at a given signal, advance with the precision of soldiers, coming out into the aisles to go through their calisthenic exercises, and then return to their seats. They know exactly where they belong, and can solve problems.

What do they do? One little fellow rises and says: "John gave Mary two dolls, and had two dolls left; how many dolls had he at first?" He then goes to the table, picks up two dolls, and says: "There are two dolls left." Then he picks up two more dolls, puts them with the first two, and shows that there are four dolls. Now, he wishes to express this on the board. He might first try to make a picture of the object, but he has already begun to use the symbols, and writes $2 + 2 = 4$. In fifteen minutes these children make more than fifteen problems, each child who makes one explaining it to the other children, showing the objects he has used. This is rational teaching, not parrot-like teaching, but genuine, beginning with what the child knows and understands, and teaching him to reason from this to the unknown. It is readily seen that there is no difficulty in the method. No person can come out of a school in which such a system is pursued and say that the children do not understand what they are doing. They learn by doing with material things, and can understand the process and the result. There is but a step from the "doing," as just illustrated, to the introduction of symbols — the figures which express *things* to us. One can see a boy; then, without the presence of the boy, he can speak of a boy; then of a picture of a boy. He can hear the spoken word "boy"; he can see the written or printed word "boy"; but when it comes to symbols, the boy may be represented by the figure "1," and the child soon learns to deal with figures as symbols of objects.

There is no teaching, no culture of the intellectual faculties, in requiring a pupil to stand and count to a hundred, a thousand, or any other number, unless illustrations should be made with objects collected by the children from all sources at their command. This keeps up a deep interest in the subject, and it helps to fix the principles in the mind. There is no reason why little children should not be taught to work with the simpler fractions just as they do with whole numbers. They enjoy the work, and take as great interest in illustrating it.

Not long since, in visiting a second-grade (second year in the primary school) room, I gave the following problem to the pupils: "If a load of wood costs three dollars and a half, what would four loads cost?"

The teacher spoke up at once, "These children have not had fractions"; but, before she had finished the sentence, nearly all hands were up, and the answer came promptly, "$14." Here is the solution they gave me: "At $3 a cord, it would cost $12, and at half a dollar a cord, four cords would cost $2; and $12 and $2 are $14." Yet these Second Reader children had never studied fractions, and the teacher was surprisingly ignorant of the information they had on the subject of fractions.

The teacher ought to find out how much the children know, instead of assuming that she knows it without inquiry.

CULTURE OF THE THINKING FACULTIES.

A question among educators is how to teach each branch so as to develop the thinking faculties. The following suggestions are submitted as having a direct bearing on this subject:

1. For every problem selected from the text-book, select three problems from outside sources.

2. Let the pupils make new or original problems, or else vary the conditions of those already given, and then solve them. The sooner pupils are put to making problems, or changing the conditions of those already given, the better they will understand the subject, and the more substantial will be their progress.

3. When the pupil comes to a new problem he tries to bring it under a form that he already knows—that is, he seeks a relationship, and, when this is once found, he proceeds to reduce it by an already familiar process.

4. Trace all problems back to primary principles.

Since the idea of number is intuitive with the race, the object of the educator should be to develop this faculty in a natural manner as the intellectual powers of the pupil are unfolded. The order of developing this subject is not different from that in teaching other branches. Evidently the very first process is that of putting together, followed immediately by separation.

Objects first attract the child's attention, and then he endeavors to put them together and to remember them, or to tell how many there are. From this it is inferred that all arithmetical teaching at first should be real or objective. Close study of child-mind points unmistakably to the following order:

1. Objects.
2. Numbering, or naming objects.
3. Names of objects as numbers.
4. Symbols of numbers.
5. Working with symbols.
6. Practical applications.

As is well known, the subject of arithmetic is frequently taught in such a manner as to stifle all efforts on the part of the pupils, and from the fact that they do not understand the processes that they mechanically perform. Instead of approaching the subject through the natural channel of objects, they are introduced at the outset to the symbolic processes, which lie beyond their reach.

All rational methods begin with objects first, then followed by the word that groups the objects into one whole, and, lastly, the symbolic number which is more general than the name of the object. Again, it should be remembered that in mental processes the mind puts together and separates, and this constitutes analysis and synthesis; and, further, after the pupil has acquired the art of reading and writing numbers, that all the operations which can be performed on numbers may be reduced to the following: Increasing, decreasing, raising to powers, and extracting roots. Furthermore, that the whole chain of mathematical reasoning is a series of comparisons, or a discovering of relations that subsist between the known factors in a given question and those that are implied. The idea of comparison lies at the foundation of Pestalozzi's system of teaching. It gives his philosophy of education its intellectual value. And upon this principle is also based the "Grube Method," which is measuring numbers in and under all possible combinations. Perhaps the author carries it too far, but it contains many valuable features, and should be thoroughly understood by every primary teacher in our country. But there are other features connected with arithmetical teaching which demand careful consideration, and first and foremost is this principle: To understand arithmetic the child must at first do the work objectively, and then put it into the symbolic form.

This meaning can best be understood by a few appropriate illustrations. The ordinary method of teaching this subject is to make the learners proficient in handling abstract numbers before introducing concrete examples; processes are accounted of more permanent value than the reasons upon which processes are based. While not undervaluing this feature of arithmetical operations, it is a violation of the natural order in which knowledge is acquired to put it first. Nature's method is that of intelligent work before generalizations can be deduced.

Suppose the pupil in his progress in arithmetic is set to learning the table for "Wine Measure." He may have studied it over till he can repeat it glibly from memory, and even give the equivalents of the different denominations in terms of the others, but the essential question of whether, in all this memorizing, the pupil's understanding is thoroughly reached, can be determined only by testing his knowledge of what he knows of the subject.

Upon the other hand, if we approach this "table" from the objective standpoint, we are struck with the simplicity as well as with the superiority of the method. Before the pupil studies the "table," let him be furnished with a gill, pint, quart, half-gallon, and a gallon measure, and a bushel of sand or a bucket of water, and then put to filling these different measures, first filling the pint cup by using the gill measure, emptying the pint into the quart measure, the quart measure into the half-gallon measure, and so on. After the gallon measure is filled it may be measured by each of the other measures, and thus, following out the philosophy in knowing one thing and comparing others with it, definite knowledge is obtained. The pupils literally do the table.

There is no question as to the superiority of this method over the memorizing one.

To learn the "Table of Long or Linear Measure," the pupil, with "foot-rule, yard-stick, or tape-line," is put to measuring and reporting results, and I do not hesitate to say that this is the only sensible way to learn this or any other table to be used in measuring any substance whatever.

From the first lessons in numbers the little child should be trained to deal with fractional numbers in their simple forms just as he is with integral numbers, the idea of fractions having been first obtained by an examination of divided objects, following the same method as the one indicated in doing the "tables." Apples divided into halves, thirds, fourths, etc., furnish excellent illustrations. It is better for the children to make the divisions. The order is: the object as a whole; secondly, the divided object; thirdly, the names of the parts; fourthly, the symbol placed on the board or slate that represents the parts; fifthly, uniting the parts again into one whole; lastly, applications.

All arithmetical problems in the elementary and advanced grades should partake largely of a business character; but vigorous drills on the fundamental rules must never be relaxed.

Many abstract exercises may give celerity in manipulating figures, but the thinking faculties are not developed. Processes without thought have but slight educational value. Repeating abstract operations in a dull lifeless manner, day after day, in the rules of arithmetic is a stultifying process, for, when the pupil once learns that $7 \times 9 = 63$, or $9 \times 7 = 63$, repeating these operations ten thousand times will give no additional information. All work should be promptly done.

MENTAL OR INTELLECTUAL ARITHMETIC

deserves more than a passing notice. It is pre-eminently the logic of the common branches, and if taught at the proper time is productive of great good. Now, all arithmetic is mental in this, that it requires, or should require, some effort of the mind to think out the method of the solution; and, furthermore, so-called practical arithmetic should always precede the mental arithmetic in a course of instruction. Mental arithmetic is more abstract than practical arithmetic; hence it should follow the latter in the earlier years of instruction, and, later on, both may be pursued simultaneously.

When mental arithmetic is pursued as a separate and an independent study, the following order of presenting and teaching the subject is recommended as one that calls into exercise the greatest number of the intellectual faculties, to wit:

The teacher will read or state the problem once, distinctly; the pupils will give the answer, indicated by raising hands; the next step, a pupil, or pupils, reproduce the question; then the analysis; and, lastly, the conclusion. Long, tedious analyses are to be avoided as a noxious pestilence.

Teaching Arithmetic.

I. Teacher.
1. Knowledge of the subject.
2. Love of the work.
3. Aptitude to teach.
4. Teach *one thing at a time.*

II. Beginners.
1. Need slates, pencils, etc.
2. Should *be taught* to observe and to think.
3. To express thoughts by symbols.

III. Primary Methods.
1. Principles and fundamental processes.
2. Fractions.
3. Denominate numbers, etc.

IV. Oral and Written.
1. Tables, etc.
2. Business forms.
3. Applications.

V. Mental Arithmetic—Steps.

CHAPTER XIII.

HEALTH AND HYGIENE.

The farmer plants corn in May or June, when the ground is warm. Should he do so in December or January, the corn would not grow. Should he leave the old stalks standing in the field, and begin to cultivate them in the warm days of spring, no life would return to them; they are dead. The stalk of corn was developed from a germ once imbedded in the kernel of the grain. With moisture from the earth, and heat from the sun, the life within the kernel manifested itself in what we call the shoot, which came to the top of the ground, grew upward, forming the stalk, and sent roots downward into the earth. During the period of its growth the farmer cultivated it, and in the fall there came a full ear, perfect, mature, ready for use.

The growth of corn is symbolical of the growth of the child from infancy to old age. If the corn is not properly cultivated, no ear is formed, and there is no kernel for use as food, or for the next year's planting. So it is with the child if he grows up without the influences and training which gradually build up character and perfect the individual.

Every human being has two lives—the mental life

and the physical life. It is of the latter I shall speak at present; not, however, to discuss at length the anatomy and physiology of the parts of the body, or to enter upon the subject of comparative physiology. According to the principles of education, we should begin with that which the child can see, can handle—that which he knows.

It is a mistake to put a text-book into the hands of school-children when it bristles with long, technical terms, hard to learn and easy to forget. Few physicians can tell the names of all the muscles of the body. Even if these names were all committed to memory, they are worth little in giving any knowledge of the subject. In talking about these things, especially to children, it seems better to describe them by pointing out their uses.

For the purpose of classifying the subject under discussion, we shall consider the body as composed of three great systems: the blood-producing, the blood-circulating, and the nervous systems. The first prepares the food for use by converting the nutritive portions into such forms as can enter the blood. Then the circulatory system carries the blood containing these nutritive particles to all parts of the body, gathers up waste matter on the way, and takes it to the lungs. In the lungs it meets the inspired air, from which it takes the purifying oxygen, giving in return the impurities which pass off with the expired air in the form of carbonic acid.

Growth is a law of our being. We grow mentally and we grow physically.

To grow, the body must have food, which includes

what we eat and what we drink. The body is sustained by proper food, pure air, exercise, rest, and sleep. But the quantity and quality must be taken into account and adapted to the conditions of the system. If you take a young colt and ride it too much, it will become "sway-backed"; if a little child is induced to walk before its bones are strong enough to support its weight, it will grow "bow-legged." It is a great mistake to overload children in any way. If they have too many studies or too long lessons in school, their minds suffer; if their bodies are overburdened, they become deformed.

So of the stomach, which is the principal digestive organ; if it is overloaded with food, it can not properly prepare it for the nourishment of the body.

Pressure upon any of the vital organs, or upon the nerves, is injurious to health.

The amount of air required by each child or older person varies from 1,000 to 2,000 cubic feet every hour, the first amount named being perhaps sufficient for small children. Suppose you are in a room 60 feet long, 25 feet wide, and 15 feet high, containing just 22,500 cubic feet of space, occupied by 80 persons, each requiring 2,000 cubic feet of air every hour. Making no allowance for the space occupied by these eighty persons and the furniture of the room, all the air in the room would be spoiled in about eight minutes— that is, the carbonic-acid gas passing off from the lungs would in that time render all the air in the room impure, unfit to breathe again. Besides, there is an insensible perspiration passing off from the body in all directions, adding to the impurity in the air. It is by such means that persons who are sick communicate contagion. There seems to be a kind of germ, which goes floating off into the air and communicating disease.

Since the air becomes so rapidly vitiated, the ventilation of school-rooms is a question of grave importance, but one which teachers too often neglect, even after they have been talked to about it day after day, week after week, month after month, and almost year after year. Even with so-called *self-registers*, the air is frequently allowed to become impure. The necessity of attention becomes even more apparent when we consider the dependence of the health of the entire body upon the perfect mutual relations between circulation and respiration, and the quality of the supplies furnished; of nutriment for distribution to all parts of the body by means of the circulation of the blood, and of air to the lungs for the purification of the blood as it passes through them on its way to the heart, there to gather fresh impetus for another journey as distributor of life-giving, and collector of dead, particles. The blood distributes its supplies for assimilation to the needs of the body, and acts as scavenger; but all this were vain did not the respiratory organs bring the oxygen in to drive out the carbonic acid, the poisonous product of decay. If ventilation is neglected, this poison remains in the blood to unite with freshly collected poison, and disease is the result, then suffering—death.

Teachers have no right to be careless in regard to this matter. Carelessness is criminality, and criminality means death. In almost every school-room there is some way to get the bad air out. Open door and windows, if no other way, and let the children run out and play, and let in pure air. If in doubt about the purity of the air in the room, step outside, inhale a few whiffs, then go into the school-room, and the contrast will tell the tale. *Try it often. Result—astonishing!*

EXERCISE.

We are told by those men who go away into the arctic regions that young seals are seen playing on the cakes of ice during the coldest days. It is natural for the young of all animals to play, and it is just as natural for a young child to play if it is in good health. It needs exercise, and needs it often. Children of larger growth need it too; it is one of the elements of life. If there are any persons so unfortunate as to be born rich enough to live without work, they are the ones who ought to practice in a gymnasium, so as to get the needed amount of physical exercise. It is an old saying that "all work and no play makes Jack a dull boy." The Greeks said that "a bow kept always strung would not shoot." Hence the bow at times must be relaxed, and the human body must have relaxation after labor. If the labor is mental, the mind must rest and the body have exercise. During study there is a greater flow of blood to the brain, and a corresponding decrease to other parts of the body. Exercise properly taken restores the equilibrium by bringing action to those parts of the body which have been at rest.

TEMPERAMENTS.

There are different physiological conditions and different mental characteristics. Suppose, for illustration, we compare two men whom we know. One of them is a perfect specimen of manhood, well rounded, tall and healthy; there is another, sharp, angular. The contrast between them is very striking. The first shows a combination of the bilious, nervous, and vital temperaments. How do we know it? The second is of a nervous-bilious temperament. The first has smooth hands, with round, tapering fingers; the other has angular hands, with knotted, bony fingers. The muscles of the first are well developed; the other is far inferior in muscular development, and needs an active out-door life to give him strength of body. Evidently they should follow different occupations. Different temperaments need different treatment; hence, teachers should study the temperaments of children. There may be one little boy who can lift fifty pounds, but should we argue from that that another who weighs as much can lift the same weight? Suppose we say to all the children in a schoolroom, regardless of their temperaments and different degrees of strength, "You must lift that fifty-pound weight." All are absurdly put to lifting the same thing in the same way, without regard to their ability.

There is a difference between trees. Compare the basswood-tree with the hickory: one is easily broken, and the other can be bent down without breaking, springing back again of itself. It is just so with children. A child who has a nervous temperament does not need to be goaded to work, but a boy of a bilious temperament may be so insensible that even a whip would not bring him into the line of march. A teacher who can understand the temperament of a child as soon as she sees it will be the successful teacher. A child who has a nervous temperament will learn rapidly, and may soon distance the others. Such as these should usually be restrained, and *never* driven. Here is a case in point: A little girl attending a school had a precocious mind, but a slight, frail body. Her mother was proud of her—anxious to display her ability. To the mother the superintendent said: "You are killing that child by pushing her too rapidly forward; let her play out-of-doors." The mother did not believe him, but urged the child onward in her studies, and with the predicted result of death.

Every teacher should read what has been written by the best authors on temperaments, and study human nature as it is, mind and body together. We have studied the mind without the body, and the body with the elements composing it, but there is a mutual dependence enabling us to judge each in some measure by the manifestation of the other. In a person having sharp, angular features, and a large, broad forehead, the nervous temperament predominates; while another with a full, plump body, a round figure, and agreeable features, is the possessor of the vital temperament. He has a large, full chest, breathing-room for his lungs, and his other vital organs are well developed. There is another, perhaps, with a gaunt, angular physiognomy, sharp features, large bones and joints, and a yellowish color of the skin, with distant, hollow-looking eyes: he is of the "bilious" or "frame-work" temperament.

Teachers, working among children, ought to manage each child according to his temperament. Not forgetting, however, that pure air, good food, and cleanliness are needed by all. 'Tis true, the bath is not a feature of school-room work, but the teacher must impress its importance upon the minds of all pupils. This applies to day-schools. In boarding-schools the teachers have the entire charge, and are in duty bound to attend to this matter.

Physiology teaches that, in the form of insensible perspiration, about five eighths of everything we take into the body passes off through the pores of the skin. For this reason clothing which is worn next to the body during the day should not be worn at night, and that worn at night should be well aired during the day. Our beds, too, should be thoroughly aired during the day, and the sleeping-rooms carefully ventilated.

Health and Hygiene—Body.

Parts.
- Bones and joints.
- Digestive organs.
- Nervous system.
- Muscles.
- Circulative system.
- Skin.

Support.
- Food.
- Exercise.
- Air.
- Rest and sleep.

Care.
- Clothing.
- Amount of air.
- Hygiene of the school-house.
- Kinds of food.
- Ventilation.
- Bathing.

CHAPTER XIV.

ONLY A BOY.

"*A very peculiar boy,* and the teacher does not understand him," is the confiding mother's verdict nine times out of ten. Teachers, have you not already formed the acquaintance of the "peculiar boy" as interpreted by his affectionate but misguided mother? Have you not analyzed the ingredients of this "peculiar boy's mind," and tested them in the educational balance? Have you not studied his mental characteristics and traced each one to its most secret hiding-place? Have you not mapped every emotion, affection, and desire, then divided and subdivided, and separated the true from the false, and ascertained by so doing that "this peculiar boy" had much in common with other boys? Did you take "this peculiar boy" mentally to pieces, and find out by an examination of his intellectual and moral mechanism that he was a well-contrived and well-made human machine, capable of doing good work if only properly regulated and directed?

But here comes the boy himself. He stands before us. He knows that he is "a peculiar boy." His mother has said so a thousand times, and he has heard her every time. She ascribes his singular disposition to changes in the weather and other like occult influences, all of which speculations assist the boy in playing a dual existence, and changing from one to the other so readily that his mother is unable to detect the deception.

I have yet to see the "peculiar boy" free from deception. Peculiarity—or his peculiarity—may assume a thousand different forms of mind and body. Not long since I had the satisfaction of watching a "peculiar boy" for fifteen minutes while his grown sister explained to the teacher some of the peculiarities of this "peculiar boy," the chief of which was that he was "unmanageable at home, and they could do nothing with him"; but she insisted that the teacher should control him without punishing him for offenses he might commit during school hours. This boy had seen the snows of ten winters, and, while his sister proceeded to enlighten the meek and patient teacher, the "peculiar boy" indulged in the following innocent sports: 1. He struck a boy near him in the side with a slate. 2. He crawled around on the floor under his desk hunting for a pin that he had dropped the day before. 3. While on the floor he put his left foot above his desk and executed a half-dozen kicking motions with that same foot, pretending, as he said, that "his foot was asleep, and he wanted to wake it." 4. Next he reached across the aisle and jerked a boy's boot-strap. He had not yet found the pin. 5. He lay flat under his desk and inspected in a very deliberate manner a joint in the floor. Well satisfied with the result of his floor observations, he crawled into the aisle, took a general survey of the surroundings, and then arose, half-bent, and tickled a boy's neck with a scrap of paper. 6. A little girl looked at him, and he pulled her hair to teach her a practical lesson. 7. He now took his seat, and, in doing so, cast furtive glances and winked at the pupils whose eyes turned toward him. 8. In less than a minute he was kicking a boy who sat directly in front of him, and, when the boy complained, he declared that he "hadn't touched the boy."

Treatment. — The above is only one instance of many that have fallen under my observation. Yet the question for the teacher to decide is what to do with such cases? Shall the boy be turned out of school because his influence contaminates others and he is far beyond the limit of parental control? Before the teacher arrives at a conclusion, all the circumstances connected with the boy's history should be carefully and conscientiously weighed.

If the teacher sees a chance to turn "his peculiarities" to a good account, he will not be slow to do so; but, if no favorable conditions are present, there is only one course for the teacher to pursue, and that is to send the intractable child to his parents.

It is a mistaken policy for school authorities to permit pupils to remain in school when they forfeit every right that is guaranteed by the laws of the State. Any citizen who behaves himself is entitled to the full enjoyment of all those absolute and acquired rights given by the Creator and by statutory enactments for his happiness and general prosperity, but with this proviso, that he will not abuse the great boon conferred, otherwise he loses all.

The "peculiar boy's disposition" is a home-made

article, and badly spoiled in the manufacture. Surrounded by an atmosphere of disorder, fitfulness, and fickleness, perhaps tainted with deception and other vices, he comes to school not to learn obedience, but to do as he pleases without restraint. When the teacher has exhausted all available resources, it is time to notify parents and school authorities that the boy's presence can not be tolerated longer in the school-room unless there is a very sudden conversion.

Remark.—I am not now speaking of those defects of the mind or of the body which render the child unfit to be in school.

THE PETTED AND SPOILED BOY.

This specimen of the human species has not so many ailments as the "peculiar boy." His case is different, symptoms are not the same, and the treatment is also dissimilar. Unless everything goes to suit his fancy, he is seen with a budding cry or a sprouting whimper on his face. Crying for things or crying because he can not have his own way, the acquired condition of his earthly existence.

The little story of "Mother, I want a piece of cake," well expresses the visible co-efficient of this boy's face. Right back of him at home is a weak-minded father or mother; probably both are afflicted with this complaint. The boy being shrewd enough to understand their weakness, and having found out that crying is the most effective plea to secure any object or the gratification of any whim which he fancies, does not hesitate to employ his skill to aid him in the furtherance of his wishes. Having managed his parents, his next effort is to capture the teacher by the same means. Of course, an experienced teacher will see through the situation at a glance, and will not be imposed upon, although the boy may be somewhat re-enforced by one or both his parents, who, by misguided zeal and moral weakness, do not clearly understand the nature of their own child and just how to treat him. A vacillating will-power and a perverse blindness to childish willfulness and deception are serious obstacles to the teacher's progress in correcting the faults of the "petted and spoiled child." But the child is in school. He is spoiled. The teacher knows it, and the pupils are not ignorant of it either. How can he be most successfully treated? Here, indeed, is a school problem! To give an answer, let us suppose a hypothetical case. The boy is a delicate little fellow physically; large blue eyes, a high, full forehead, flaxen hair, a slender frame, a milky complexion produced from eating rich and highly seasoned indigestible food, a nervous temperament, with only a slight admixture with the motive and vital temperaments. Picture him before you as the "petted and spoiled boy"!

As I take it, the first step is to gain this child's confidence. A dog knows how to approach a stranger and win his kindness. There is some avenue open to this child's better nature. A little judicious digging and spading around will enable the teacher to find it. Make no mistakes, but strike the right lead at first. Teacher, don't dig till you are sure, and you will capture him. He is taken as the farmer's wife catches a mole in the garden. She waits and watches till the mole begins to dig near the top of the ground; then she digs with the spade just ahead of the mole, and instantly just behind him, tossing him out on top of the ground. She never mistakes the hour, the place, or the means to capture the mole. By a little judicious and faithful work the teacher can capture the "petted and spoiled boy," and have him completely under her control.

The child I have presented is of such peculiar mental and physical organization as to be very susceptible to appeals made to his higher emotional nature through his intellectual faculties. Naturally, the child of the delicately-wrought nervous temperament is not cruel and brutal, yet he may be sly and crafty. Subdue or lull into repose the vicious tendencies and stimulate the nobler ones to increased activity. It may be necessary to excite his self-approbation or his desire to have others—and especially his teacher and schoolmates—think well of him. Whatever influence is proper should be brought to bear upon him to move him in the line of right conduct.

Above all, the teacher must be honest with the child. No deception will answer the purpose. Children read motives, actions, and words intuitively.

Since the "petted and spoiled child" may be of any temperament, let us extend our inquiries.

For present purposes children may be classified into three groups, namely, the good, the medium, and the bad.

The first group will give but little or no trouble at home or in school. They behave properly, and only in rare instances is one of this class to be reproved.

But the middle group, composing the vast concourse of children, is highly susceptible to good and bad influences. These are the children standing "on slippery places." Environments make or unmake them. If started in the right direction, and carefully watched till habits are formed and fixed, they will move onward through life as honorable and useful members of society. When passion is strong, the will-power weak, reason only partially developed, and the habits in process of formation, then it is that the child needs the steady hand of the teacher to lead him along the dangerous pathway.

Through affection for the teacher the wayward boy becomes obedient, and most cheerfully submits to those rules and regulations of school which are established for his well-being. Without this spirit of love he submits only from sheer necessity.

The incorrigible or untamed child is hard to control; but even the most vicious always have some good traits. These traits should be found out and then developed. The human face is always a true index of the character. Profoundly versed in faces, and knowing how to turn everything to the best account, the teacher is skillful only in proportion as he can change the natural tendencies from viciousness to uprightness. Education does not change the character; it changes the direction—the life. It causes the individual to change his powers from one mode of thinking, feeling, and acting to another. The motives are different. Placing before the pupil a better set of motives, and letting these impel him to action in a newer and higher direction, is the chief value of a right education.

To pluck out or displace a bad motive, and to put a better one in its place, is the highest duty a teacher is ever called upon to perform. Hunt, therefore, for the good qualities in the child's nature. Develop these, and the worst case of "petted and spoiled" may be cured.

FIDGETY BOY.

No description of this irritation of the school-room is needed. He is too well known.

The first step is to ascertain the cause of this state of uncontrollableness. It may depend originally upon two conditions of the body, namely, an inherited nervousness, or from a large preponderance of life and animal spirits in the system, such as usually accompany a full development of the sanguine-vital temperaments; or it may not be dependent upon either of these, but merely capricious willfulness. In any event, probe the case to the bottom, and then base your action upon the result of your examination.

I will briefly indicate the remedies for these three distinct types of "fidgets."

1. Keep cool, and never become flurried or excited. Speak quietly, gently, in the school-room. Thus you insensibly tone down the highly wrought nervous children under your tuition. Your influence should soothe, not irritate, the delicate children who are so susceptible that every sound strikes a thousand tense nerves in their bodies.

Here, also, is an excellent opportunity for the teacher to study himself, and to note particularly what effect he produces upon the minds of his pupils.

2. A pupil having a large supply of blood in his body needs pure air and out-door exercise. Confined in a school-room, he longs to get out and to get away.

Nature indicates that he should run around. Let him do something for you. Send him on errands. Such exercise will purify his blood, and will keep him out of mischief. Such pupils need work-shops as well as study-rooms.

3. The last case is managed easily. *Don't permit it!*

THE SULLEN BOY.

The infant is born into the world with capabilities that may be developed. Everything he will ever know must be learned. His tendencies, or the "bent of his mind," are to be guided and directed. Early in life the child is not supposed to know in all cases what is best for him to do or not to do. Experience teaches lessons after many failures. Proper education is just as needful for the mind as food, air, clothing, and exercise are for the body. To educate is, in one sense, to put the mind in that condition so that it may gather knowledge, arrange it, classify it, and have it ready for use; and the effort put forth in getting knowledge gives additional power and skill to overcome other difficulties.

The sullen or stubborn boy is sometimes met with in the school-room.

Symptoms. — For some reason the pupil takes it into his head that he will not do anything the teacher requests him to do. When spoken to, he replies frequently by rolling his eyes in an indifferent sort of a way about the school-room. When requested to move, he sits still in dogged silence. If threatened, he is equally indifferent. Threats and coaxing have precisely the same effect—sublime and haughty contempt! It is no more nor less than his will-power acting through stubbornness in opposition to the teacher's will.

Remedial Agents.—There are some old-fashioned teachers who claim that a keen, tough switch possesses excellent virtues in the hands of an able-bodied teacher on such occasions. In a very few cases it may do good, but let the switch be used very sparingly.

An Anecdote.—On one occasion a miss of fifteen flatly refused to recite her lesson or answer any question which her teacher asked her.

She was excused and took her seat. At the next recitation she sat quietly, the teacher paying no attention to her whatever. Thus the day wore away. Next morning she came to school in due time, meanwhile chatting lively with her classmates. School was called. At the proper time she took her place with her class, ready for recitation. The teacher kindly and pleasantly informed her that, till she could act in a becoming manner, she would not recite to him, and, since she had voluntarily chosen to deprive herself of the privileges of school, the proper place for her would be at home; she was therefore excused. But he added that, if at any time she concluded to comply with the rules and regulations of the school, she might return. Three hours later she came back. The teacher had conquered.

Time I regard as the essential element in outgeneraling the "sullen boy." When the question of supremacy of will-power is once decided, the question is settled.

THE FIGHTING AND SWEARING BOY.

Nearly all boys will fight and swear. There are few exceptions. Of course, a boy may fight in self-defense, or to protect another person; or, under intense excitement, he may use language more emphatic than refined:

it is not my purpose to discuss rare and exceptional cases.

The right to protect one's self in his person, reputation, and property, is recognized as an instinct of our nature, and all persons act upon this right, with the exception of those who advocate the non-resistance doctrine.

But the "fighting and swearing boy" is an intolerable nuisance in the school. As a disturber of the peace he has few equals and no superiors. He takes special delight in creating disturbances, and in getting others into fights and broils, and then in glorying in their discomfiture. One noisy, fighting, swearing boy will contaminate an entire school, and nullify the teacher's efforts, unless some plan is adopted whereby his course of conduct is turned into better channels.

Whenever the teacher finds such a case in school, there should be no waste of time in setting about a method of correcting him. If his instincts are low and brutal, and through force of habit at home he has acquired a quarrelsome and fighting disposition, there is no higher element in his nature to appeal to than that of overcoming physical force with physical force. It is the same principle that enables Conklin to tame and subdue the lion. A combination of mind and muscle exercising sway over a lower order of mind may be the means of elevating the latter; yet the motives are certainly not those of the nobler kind.

Frequently it happens that the "fighting boy" has a high sense of honor, and, having established his reputation as a pugilist, he is exceedingly desirous of maintaining the title, at no little personal sacrifice. If the boy be of such a character, an appeal to his manhood is perhaps the most effectual way of reaching him, and thereby reforming his habits. Wrong notions of true bravery have done much to foster fighting, and to give it an air of respectability in many sections of our country.

The toleration of prize-fighting and pugilistic exhibitions generally, and the greediness with which accounts of such matters are devoured by no small portion of the public, help to foster the fighting spirit among schoolboys. Doubtless the statement is measurably true that even the most highly enlightened and civilized communities still retain many traces of barbarism. The English, Irish, and a very large portion of the Americans, have combativeness and destructiveness largely developed, and they are too frequently impelled to work off this superfluous energy through their fists and feet.

By his influence, inculcating higher notions of life and the dignity of true manhood, and the brutal and disgraceful features connected with fighting, the teacher can do much toward creating a public sentiment in a community against fighting.

"That man only is truly brave who fears nothing so much as doing a shameful action, and that dares resolutely and undauntedly go where his duty, how dangerous soever it is, may call him."

By reference to noble deeds and virtuous actions, placing higher incentives before the minds of children, they may be taught to emulate the true, the good, and the honorable of earth. Hence, by strong, earnest, honest, continuous effort, the teacher may change, in almost every instance, "*the fighting and swearing boy*" into a quiet, orderly, and industrious pupil. Precept, practice, correct judgment properly applied, will effect more toward turning the baser metal into gold than the brightest visions of the alchemist's dreams.

THE LAZY BOY.

There is a prevailing opinion that no little child is lazy, and, as an evidence of this fact, the activity and sportiveness of all young animals are referred to as confirmatory of this belief. While it is admitted, and with a considerable degree of plausibility likewise, that healthy young animals really enjoy themselves in various ways, yet I am not fully convinced, from all the evidence now before me, that the analogy between animals and children will bear close and impartial investigation. Be that matter as it may, if all young children are not lazy, a considerable number " are born into the world with an astonishing amount of tiredness fastened upon them."

Laziness is a disinclination to work, either with the mind or body, and some cases of it—whether hereditary or acquired, it matters not—are actually found in school. Upon physiological conditions, it is readily understood how and why a rapidly growing child may be lazy. Perhaps it requires all the vitality which he possesses to satisfy the physical demands of his system. Laziness, unless it be a newly manufactured article, depends largely upon temperamental conditions. These conditions can, through a series of years, be modified, but not entirely obliterated. An inquiry should be made here as to whether the laziness is primary or secondary: primary when it is inbred and inborn, and secondary when it accompanies rapidly growing childhood. The second phase passes away usually in the course of a few years. The teacher can do little with laziness unless he goes at once to the roots of the disease. To tell a child that he is lazy oftentimes does more harm than good.

1. Occasionally the school-room feature of the case is relieved by inducing the child " to go to bed early and to sleep nine or ten hours out of the twenty-four."

2. A pupil may appear dull, stupid, and lazy, when in reality he is slow to apprehend new things, or it is with difficulty that he can turn from one subject to another. In this instance he is usually classed as a " lazy, slow boy."

3. Plenty of exercise in the open air is a wonderful invigorator.

4. Light, easily digested, nutritious food aids mental activity.

5. Laziness, or dullness, or fatness, can not be whipped out of a child any more than learning can be whipped into him.

THE LYING BOY.

All persons having a high regard for truthfulness agree that it is better to speak the truth, though the penalty of death be incurred, than to prevaricate. The conflicting motives are present and future happiness.

Lying is so detestable that ancients and moderns are unanimous in condemning it.

" Liars are the cause of all the sins and crimes in the world."—*Epictetus.*

" A lie has no legs, and can not stand; but it has wings, and can fly far and wide."— *Warburton.*

"Sin has many tools, but a lie is the handle which fits them all."—*Holmes.*

"Every brave man shuns more than death the shame of lying."—*Corneille.*

"None but cowards lie."—*Murphy.*

"When first found in a lie, talk to him of it as a strange, monstrous matter, and so shame him out of it."—*Locke.*

The educator deals with human nature just as he finds it in every-day life. While he may create lofty ideals, and strive to reach them himself and to induce his pupils to go as far or farther, yet it is mostly with commonplace persons that his life is spent.

In a school, as in a community, a public sentiment can be created, and that sentiment shapes, in a very considerable degree, popular opinion.

In a community known for fair dealing in business transactions, and whose people are truthful, and their words fitly chosen and properly spoken, a liar stands a poor chance, because he is readily known in his true character as a dishonest man. Not unfrequently a liar has found himself so out of place among honest and veracious people that he has been known "to turn over a new leaf and commence telling the truth," and in due time to establish a fair reputation as a good citizen. This may be ascribed mostly to the moral standard of the community in which the prevaricator lived.

What is true of a community or neighborhood is likewise true of a school. In effecting a general reformation, the teacher is advised first to create a moral sentiment, and, in an effective way, bring the public opinion of the school up to that standard.

It is a well-known fact that children generally prefer to have the good-will of their schoolmates rather than their ill-will. Thus the many are united as a band to uphold the unsteady one. One little kernel of confidence planted in a boy's soul oftentimes works wonders in his whole life. To know that he is trusted, and that there are those who grieve and are sad at thought of his bad actions, has been the means of lifting many a pupil to a higher and purer life.

Here, again, the teacher's daily life, as he lives it, is the most potent factor. It was the respect that the "boys of Rugby" had for the open, manly character of Dr. Arnold that kept them from lying to him. I believe that nearly all children may be influenced similarly.

ILLUSTRATION.

Twenty-five years ago there lived in a Western town a boy ten years old. His father worked but little, and the mother "took in washing" to get food for her children. The boy—the eldest child—was called a "thief and a liar" by everybody. Good people would not let their children play with this "vagabond," as he was frequently called.

A stranger was induced by a few prominent citizens to open a select school in this town, but he was cautioned by several responsible persons not to admit this notorious boy to school: First, he would spoil better children; and, secondly, his parents were unable to pay his tuition. Strange as it may appear, the stranger decided that, if this boy should come to school, he would admit him, for a while at least.

The first week of school came and went, and the

"notorious boy" was still running the streets; but the second Monday morning there he was, sure enough, ragged, dirty, bright, and noisy—a regular "Ishmaelite," so to speak, among the other boys. School being called, he came in and took a front seat. Presently the teacher went to him and asked him very quietly and very pleasantly "if he wanted to come to school." "You bet," was the emphatic reply. The boy, apparently, received little attention that day, yet the teacher had taken a pretty correct measure of him before school closed in the afternoon. Enough to say that on Wednesday this boy was sent on an errand to purchase "chalk for the blackboard," a little service that he performed faithfully, and, by Friday night, he was behaving himself as well as any other pupil in school.

Next Monday morning he was at school early, and helped the teacher make the fire in the stove. It was then and there that that boy made the following manly confession:

"Teacher," he said, "everybody says that I lie and steal, and that I am a mean boy; nobody trusts me but you. I want to be good, and won't you like me if I am a good boy?" With tears glistening in his eyes, the teacher took the child by the hand, and then said "Yes."

Years passed by. This boy learned a good trade, became an industrious citizen, and, at last accounts, was the possessor of a pleasant home, surrounded by an interesting family.

The reader must not infer that all similar cases can be cured in this way, but I am firmly of the opinion that a very large percentage of cases may be reformed under proper and judicious treatment.

The old adage, "Give a dog a bad name and hang him," is just as true of people. When self-respect is lost, all is lost, and there is nothing left to build on, or to build to.

One of the worst phases of lying is that in which one pupil tells a deliberate falsehood in regard to another pupil. When an offense of this character is committed, the offender should suffer for it; and also when a pupil lies and willfully persists in the lie afterward. In such cases it is best to inform the parent or guardian of the child's conduct. This delicate duty frequently requires the rarest tact upon the part of the teacher to avoid giving offense to the parent.

The precise nature of the punishment to be inflicted must be determined mainly from the circumstances connected with each case as it arises.

OTHER BOYS.

There are yet other peculiar boys that deserve a passing notice.

Who has not seen the "sharp, sly, foxy boy"? An innocent look, yet beneath it all so many signs that told the story of his character. And "the noisy boy," too! Not mischievous, only noisy! He, too, is to be tamed down. A quiet, dignified teacher can calm him easily.

The real "saucy boy," who delights in worrying the teacher, and whose memory is exceedingly treacherous, is generally more than a match for a peevish, fretful teacher. He is continually "forgetting," "speaking without permission," or in some way or other troubling the teacher. What he should not say, he says, and he seldom does the right thing at the right time.

As such cases are not hard to manage if the teacher keeps her temper, we dismiss them to introduce the "*scary* boy"!

Some children are excessively timid; so timid, indeed, that, if the teacher only look at them, they cry. I was met on the street recently by a man who said "that his little boy had been in school two weeks, and yet the teacher would not let him recite a lesson." "Strange," I replied, "but there is a mistake somewhere. Let us hunt it up." He did not have time, but I went at once to the room.

The child was there. He had not recited a lesson. If the teacher but looked at him, he cried aloud; if she stepped in the direction of his seat, he would scream with all his might. What could the teacher do? She was a lady of the kindest disposition; her children loved her, and by all of them she was called their "school-mother." But this particular little fellow was "*scary*"; it appeared to be born in him, and he could not help it. Upon my advice he was taken away from school.

Usually, timid children soon get over their sensitiveness, especially if the teacher treats them with kindness and makes them feel that they have nothing to fear.

In dealing with "hard or exceptional cases," there are two ideas the teacher must ever keep in view: 1. The good of the individual pupil. 2. The welfare of the school. The welfare of the many must not be sacrificed for the few or the one. Back of sympathy—back of all devices—is the question of obedience. To this, as the highest tribunal, all cases of disobedience, if they will not yield to milder remedies, must be brought.

The good teacher always keeps his reserve power well in hand, and those who will not submit must suffer the consequences of their own folly. One of the most lasting lessons a system of education can inculcate is, that transgression brings its own punishment.

The teacher, standing as it were at the threshold of the child's life, sees two paths widely divergent, and along which the child must choose one or the other and travel. One leads out into the street—to vicious habits, lying, theft, drunkenness, disgrace, poverty, and wretchedness; a life without an aim, without a purpose; a wretched failure! The other conducts to success in business, secures the confidence and approbation of mankind, elevates the race, dignifies humanity, and brings its possessor happiness and contentment in old age.

With such conceptions of life the true teacher works to realize his highest ideals, and, as his race is run and he falls at last, he points out the path to a more glorious reward for the "wayward boys."

Only a Boy.

1. A very peculiar boy.
2. The petted and spoiled boy.
3. The fidgety boy.
4. The sullen boy.
5. The fighting and swearing boy.
6. The lazy boy.
7. The lying boy.
8. Other boys.

THE END.

D. APPLETON AND COMPANY'S PUBLICATIONS.

NEW VOLUMES IN THE INTERNATIONAL EDUCATION SERIES.

BIBLIOGRAPHY OF EDUCATION. By WILL S. MONROE, A. B., Department of Pedagogy and Psychology, State Normal School, Westfield, Mass. $2.00.

This book will prove of great use to normal schools, training schools for teachers, and to educational lecturers and all special students seeking to acquaint themselves with the literature of any particular department. It will be of especial value to librarians in the way of assisting them to answer two questions : (*a*) What books has this library on any special educational theme ? (*b*) What books ought it to obtain to complete its collection in that theme ?

FROEBEL'S EDUCATIONAL LAWS FOR ALL TEACHERS. By JAMES L. HUGHES, Inspector of Schools, Toronto. $1.50.

The aim of this book is to give a simple exposition of the most important principles of Froebel's educational philosophy, and to make suggestions regarding the application of these principles to the work of the schoolroom in teaching and training. It will answer the question often propounded, How far beyond the kindergarten can Froebel's principles be successfully applied ?

SCHOOL MANAGEMENT AND SCHOOL METHODS. By Dr. J. BALDWIN, Professor of Pedagogy in the University of Texas ; Author of " Elementary Psychology and Education " and " Psychology applied to the Art of Teaching." $1.50.

This is eminently an everyday working book for teachers; practical, suggestive, inspiring. It presents clearly the best things achieved, and points the way to better things. School organization, school control, and school methods are studies anew from the standpoint of pupil betterment. The teacher is led to create the ideal school, embodying all that is best in school work, and stimulated to endeavor earnestly to realize the ideal.

PRINCIPLES AND PRACTICE OF TEACHING. By JAMES JOHONNOT. Revised by SARAH EVANS JOHONNOT. $1.50.

This book embodies in a compact form the results of the wide experience and careful reflection of an enthusiastic teacher and school supervisor. Mr. Johonnot as an educational reformer helped thousands of struggling teachers who had brought over the rural school methods into village school work. He made life worth living to them. His help, through the pages of this book, will aid other thousands in the same struggle to adopt the better methods that are possible in the graded school. The teacher who aspires to better his instruction will read this book with profit.

D. APPLETON AND COMPANY, NEW YORK.

D. APPLETON AND COMPANY'S PUBLICATIONS.

JAMES SULLY'S WORKS.

STUDIES OF CHILDHOOD. 8vo. Cloth, $2.50.

An ideal popular scientific book. These studies proceed on sound scientific lines in accounting for the mental manifestations of children, yet they require the reader to follow no laborious train of reasoning; and the reader who is in search of entertainment merely will find it in the quaint sayings and doings with which the volume abounds.

CHILDREN'S WAYS. Being Selections from the Author's "Studies of Childhood," and some additional matter. 12mo. Cloth, $1.50.

This work is mainly a condensation of the author's previous book, "Studies of Childhood," but considerable new matter is added. The material that Mr. Sully supplies is the most valuable of recent contributions on the psychological phases of child study.

TEACHER'S HAND-BOOK OF PSYCHOLOGY. On the Basis of "Outlines of Psychology." Abridged by the Author for the use of Teachers, Schools, Reading Circles, and Students generally. Fourth edition, rewritten and enlarged. 12mo. Cloth, $1.50.

"The present edition has been carefully revised throughout, largely rewritten, and enlarged by about fifty pages. While seeking to preserve the original character of the book as an *introduction*, I have felt it necessary, in view of the fact that our best training colleges for secondary teachers are now making a serious study of psychology, to amplify somewhat and bring up to date the exposition of scientific principles. I have also touched upon those recent developments of experimental psychology which have concerned themselves with the measurement of the simpler mental processes, and which promise to have important educational results by supplying accurate tests of children's abilities."—*From the Author's Preface.*

OUTLINES OF PSYCHOLOGY, *with Special Reference to the Theory of Education.* A Text-Book for Colleges. Crown 8vo. Cloth, $3.00.

ILLUSIONS. A Psychological Study. 12mo, 372 pages. Cloth, $1.50.

PESSIMISM. A History and a Criticism. Second edition. 8vo. 470 pages and Index. Cloth, $4.00.

THE HUMAN MIND. A Text-Book of Psychology. Two volumes. 8vo. Cloth, $5.00.

D. APPLETON AND COMPANY, NEW YORK.

D. APPLETON AND COMPANY'S PUBLICATIONS.

PUNCTUATION. With Chapters on Hyphenization, Capitalization, Spelling, etc. By F. HORACE TEALL, author of "English Compound Words and Phrases," etc. 16mo. Cloth, $1.00.

"The rules and directions for the use of the various marks of punctuation are brief, clear, and founded on common sense. They are calculated to assist, and there seems no danger that they will confuse."—*Boston Herald.*

"It seems to be one of the most sensible and practical works on the subject that has come under notice."—*Cleveland Plain Dealer.*

"A work that can be safely commended for its simplification of a subject that often puzzles others besides literary workers who are called upon to decide between conflicting theories as to punctuation."—*Philadelphia Press.*

FRENCH STUMBLING-BLOCKS AND ENGLISH STEPPING-STONES. By FRANCIS TARVER, M. A., late Senior French Master at Eton College. 12mo. Cloth, $1.00.

"A most valuable book for advanced students of French as well as beginners. . . . The book is one of the most useful of the many good books that appear on this subject."—*San Francisco Bulletin.*

"One can hardly commend it too highly."—*Boston Herald.*

"A work which will be of great help to the reader and student of French, and which fully meets the promise of its title."—*Chicago Evening Post.*

DON'T; or, Directions for avoiding Improprieties in Conduct and Common Errors of Speech. By CENSOR. *Parchment-Paper Edition*, square 18mo, 30 cents. *Vest-Pocket Edition*, cloth, flexible, gilt edges, red lines, 30 cents. *Boudoir Edition* (with a new chapter designed for young people), cloth, gilt, 30 cents. 138th thousand.

"Don't" deals with manners at the table, in the drawing-room, and in public, with taste in dress, with personal habits, with common mistakes in various situations in life, and with ordinary errors of speech.

WHAT TO DO. A Companion to "Don't." By Mrs. OLIVER BELL BUNCE. Small 18mo, cloth, gilt, uniform with *Boudoir Edition* of "Don't," 30 cents.

A dainty little book, containing helpful and practical explanations of social usages and rules.

ERRORS IN THE USE OF ENGLISH. By the late WILLIAM B. HODGSON, LL. D., Fellow of the College of Preceptors, and Professor of Political Economy in the University of Edinburgh. 12mo. Cloth, $1.50.

D. APPLETON AND COMPANY, NEW YORK.

D. APPLETON AND COMPANY'S PUBLICATIONS.

PROF. JOSEPH LE CONTE'S WORKS.

ELEMENTS OF GEOLOGY. A Text-Book for Colleges and for the General Reader. With upward of 900 Illustrations. New and enlarged edition. 8vo. Cloth, $4.00.

"Besides preparing a comprehensive text-book, suited to present demands, Professor Le Conte has given us a volume of great value as an exposition of the subject, thoroughly up to date. The examples and applications of the work are almost entirely derived from this country, so that it may be properly considered an American geology. We can commend this work without qualification to all who desire an intelligent acquaintance with geological science, as fresh, lucid, full, and authentic, the result of devoted study and of long experience in teaching."—*Popular Science Monthly.*

EVOLUTION AND ITS RELATION TO RELIGIOUS THOUGHT. With numerous Illustrations. New and enlarged edition. 12mo. Cloth, $1.50.

"The questions suggested by this title must weigh with more or less persistence on the mind of every intelligent and liberal thinker. . . . The man who can keep his science and his religion in two boxes, either of which may be opened separately, is to be congratulated. Many of us can not, and his peace of mind we can not attain. Therefore every contribution toward a means of clearer vision is most welcome, above all when it comes from one who knows the ground on which he stands, and has conquered his right to be there. . . . Professor Le Conte is a man in whom reverence and imagination have not become desiccated by a scientific atmosphere, but flourish, in due subordination and control, to embellish and vivify his writings. Those who know them have come to expect a peculiar alertness of mind and freshness of method in any new work by this author, whether his conclusions be such as they are ready to receive or not."—*The Nation.*

"Professor Le Conte is a devout Christian believer; he is also a radical evolutionist. . . . There is no better book than this for a student to read in order to get a broad and general view of the theory of evolution and the evidence by which it is supported."—*Christian Union.*

RELIGION AND SCIENCE. A Series of Sunday Lectures on the Relation of Natural and Revealed Religion, or the Truths revealed in Nature and Scripture. 12mo. Cloth, $1.50.

"We commend the book cordially to the regard of all who are interested in whatever pertains to the discussion of these grave questions, and especially to those who desire to examine closely the strong foundations on which the Christian faith is reared."—*Boston Journal.*

SIGHT: An Exposition of the Principles of Monocular and Binocular Vision. With Illustrations. 12mo. Cloth, $1.50.

"Professor Le Conte has long been known as an original investigator in this department; all that he gives us is treated with a master hand. It is pleasant to find an American book that can rank with the very best of foreign books on this subject."—*The Nation.*

D. APPLETON AND COMPANY, NEW YORK.

SELF-EDUCATION.

Punctuation.
With Chapters on Hyphenization, Capitalization, Spelling, etc. By F. HORACE TEALL. 16mo. Cloth, $1.00.

Slips of Tongue and Pen.
By J. H. LONG, M. A. 12mo. Cloth, 60 cents.

Grammar without a Master.
The English Grammar of William Cobbett. Carefully revised, annotated, and indexed by ALFRED AYRES. 18mo. Cloth, $1.00.

The Orthoëpist.
A Pronouncing Manual. Revised and enlarged edition. 292 pages. By ALFRED AYRES. 18mo. Cloth, $1.25.

The Verbalist.
A Manual devoted to Brief Discussions of the Right and the Wrong Use of Words. By ALFRED AYRES. 18mo. Cloth, $1.25.

The Correspondent.
By JAMES WOOD DAVIDSON. Small 12mo. Cloth, 60 cents.

Errors in the Use of English.
By W. B. HODGSON, LL. D. American revised edition. 12mo. Cloth, $1.50.

D. APPLETON AND COMPANY, NEW YORK.

INTERNATIONAL EDUCATION SERIES.

12mo, cloth, uniform binding.

THE INTERNATIONAL EDUCATION SERIES was projected for the purpose of bringing together in orderly arrangement the best writings, new and old, upon educational subjects, and presenting a complete course of reading and training for teachers generally. It is edited by WILLIAM T. HARRIS, LL. D., United States Commissioner of Education, who has contributed for the different volumes in the way of introduction, analysis, and commentary. The volumes are tastefully and substantially bound in uniform style.

VOLUMES NOW READY.

1. **The Philosophy of Education.** By JOHANN K. F. ROSENKRANZ, Doctor of Theology and Professor of Philosophy, University of Königsberg. Translated by ANNA C. BRACKETT. Second edition, revised, with Commentary and complete Analysis. $1.50.
2. **A History of Education.** By F. V. N. PAINTER, A. M., Professor of Modern Languages and Literature, Roanoke College, Va. $1.50.
3. **The Rise and Early Constitution of Universities.** WITH A SURVEY OF MEDIÆVAL EDUCATION. By S. S. LAURIE, LL. D., Professor of the Institutes and History of Education, University of Edinburgh. $1.50.
4. **The Ventilation and Warming of School Buildings.** By GILBERT B. MORRISON, Teacher of Physics and Chemistry, Kansas City High School. $1.00.
5. **The Education of Man.** By FRIEDRICH FROEBEL. Translated and annotated by W. N. HAILMANN, A. M., Superintendent of Public Schools, La Porte, Ind. $1.50.
6. **Elementary Psychology and Education.** By JOSEPH BALDWIN, A. M., LL. D., author of "The Art of School Management." $1.50.
7. **The Senses and the Will.** (Part I of "THE MIND OF THE CHILD.") By W. PREYER, Professor of Physiology in Jena. Translated by H. W. BROWN, Teacher in the State Normal School at Worcester. Mass. $1.50.
8. **Memory: What it is and How to Improve it.** By DAVID KAY, F. R. G. S., author of "Education and Educators," etc. $1.50.
9. **The Development of the Intellect.** (Part II of "THE MIND OF THE CHILD.") By W. PREYER, Professor of Physiology in Jena. Translated by H. W. BROWN. $1.50.
10. **How to Study Geography.** A Practical Exposition of Methods and Devices in Teaching Geography which apply the Principles and Plans of Ritter and Guyot. By FRANCIS W. PARKER, Principal of the Cook County (Illinois) Normal School. $1.50.
11. **Education in the United States:** Its History from the Earliest Settlements. By RICHARD G. BOONE, A. M., Professor of Pedagogy, Indiana University. $1.50.
12. **European Schools; OR, WHAT I SAW IN THE SCHOOLS OF GERMANY, FRANCE, AUSTRIA, AND SWITZERLAND.** By L. R. KLEMM, Ph. D., Principal of the Cincinnati Technical School. Fully illustrated. $2.00.
13. **Practical Hints for the Teachers of Public Schools.** By GEORGE HOWLAND, Superintendent of the Chicago Public Schools. $1.00.
14. **Pestalozzi: His Life and Work.** By ROGER DE GUIMPS. Authorized Translation from the second French edition, by J. RUSSELL, B. A. With an Introduction by Rev. R. H. QUICK, M. A. $1.50.
15. **School Supervision.** By J. L. PICKARD, LL. D. $1.00.
16. **Higher Education of Women in Europe.** By HELENE LANGE, Berlin. Translated and accompanied by comparative statistics by L. R. KLEMM. $1.00.
17. **Essays on Educational Reformers.** By ROBERT HERBERT QUICK, M. A., Trinity College, Cambridge. Only authorized edition of the work as rewritten in 1890. $1.50.
18. **A Text-Book in Psychology.** By JOHANN FRIEDRICH HERBART. Translated by MARGARET K. SMITH. $1.00.

THE INTERNATIONAL EDUCATION SERIES.—(Continued.)

19. **Psychology Applied to the Art of Teaching.** By JOSEPH BALDWIN, A. M., LL. D. $1.50.
20. **Rousseau's Émile; OR, TREATISE ON EDUCATION.** Translated and annotated by W. H. PAYNE, Ph. D., LL. D. $1.50.
21. **The Moral Instruction of Children.** By FELIX ADLER. $1.50.
22. **English Education in the Elementary and Secondary Schools.** By ISAAC SHARPLESS, LL. D., President of Haverford College. $1.00.
23. **Education from a National Standpoint.** By ALFRED FOUILLÉE. $1.50.
24. **Mental Development of the Child.** By W. PREYER, Professor of Physiology in Jena. Translated by H. W. BROWN. $1.00.
25. **How to Study and Teach History.** By B. A. HINSDALE, Ph. D., LL. D., University of Michigan. $1.50.
26. **Symbolic Education.** A COMMENTARY ON FROEBEL'S "MOTHER-PLAY." By SUSAN E. BLOW. $1.50.
27. **Systematic Science Teaching.** By EDWARD GARDNIER HOWE. $1.50.
28. **The Education of the Greek People.** By THOMAS DAVIDSON. $1.50.
29. **The Evolution of the Massachusetts Public-School System.** By G. H. MARTIN, A. M. $1.50.
30. **Pedagogics of the Kindergarten.** By FRIEDRICH FROEBEL. 12mo. $1.50.
31. **The Mottoes and Commentaries of Freidrich Froebel's Mother-Play.** By SUSAN E. BLOW and HENRIETTA R. ELIOT. $1.50.
32. **The Songs and Music of Froebel's Mother-Play.** By SUSAN E. BLOW. $1.50.
33. **The Psychology of Number, and its Application to Methods of Teaching Arithmetic.** By JAMES A. MCLELLAN, A. M., and JOHN DEWEY, Ph. D. $1.50.
34. **Teaching the Language-Arts.** SPEECH, READING, COMPOSITION. By B. A. HINSDALE, Ph. D., LL. D. $1.00.
35. **The Intellectual and Moral Development of the Child.** PART I. Containing Chapters on PERCEPTION, EMOTION, MEMORY, IMAGINATION, and CONSCIOUSNESS. By GABRIEL COMPAYRÉ. Translated from the French by MARY E. WILSON. $1.50.
36. **Herbart's A B C of Sense-Perception, and Introductory Works.** By WILLIAM J. ECKOFF, Ph. D., Pd. D. $1.50.
37. **Psychologic Foundations of Education.** By WILLIAM T. HARRIS, A. M, LL. D. $1.50.
38. **The School System of Ontario.** By the Hon. GEORGE W. ROSS, LL. D., Minister of Education for the Province of Ontario. $1.00.
39. **Principles and Practice of Teaching.** By JAMES JOHONNOT. $1.50.
40. **School Management and School Methods.** By JOSEPH BALDWIN. $1.50.
41. **Froebel's Educational Laws for all Teachers.** By JAMES L. HUGHES, Inspector of Schools, Toronto. $1.50.
42. **Bibliography of Education.** By WILL S. MONROE, A. B. $2.00.
43. **The Study of the Child.** By A. R. TAYLOR, Ph. D. $1.50.
44. **Education by Development.** By FRIEDRICH FROEBEL. Translated by JOSEPHINE JARVIS. $1.50.
45. **Letters to a Mother.** By SUSAN E. BLOW. $1.50.
46. **Montaigne's The Education of Children.** Translated by L. E. RECTOR, Ph. D. $1.00.
47. **The Secondary School System of Germany.** By FREDERICK E. BOLTON. $1.50.

OTHER VOLUMES IN PREPARATION.

D. APPLETON AND COMPANY, NEW YORK.

D. APPLETON AND COMPANY'S PUBLICATIONS.

THE ANTHROPOLOGICAL SERIES.

NOW READY.

THE BEGINNINGS OF ART. By ERNST GROSSE, Professor of Philosophy in the University of Freiburg A new volume in the Anthropological Series, edited by Professor Frederick Starr. Illustrated. 12mo. Cloth, $1.75.

"This book can not fail to interest students of every branch of art, while the general reader who will dare to take hold of it will have his mind broadened and enriched beyond what he would conceive a work of many times its dimensions might effect."—*Brooklyn Eagle.*

"The volume is clearly written, and should prove a popular exposition of a deeply interesting theme."—*Philadelphia Public Ledger.*

WOMAN'S SHARE IN PRIMITIVE CULTURE. By OTIS TUFTON MASON, A. M., Curator of the Department of Ethnology in the United States National Museum. With numerous Illustrations. 12mo. Cloth, $1.75.

"A most interesting *résumé* of the revelations which science has made concerning the habits of human beings in primitive times, and especially as to the place, the duties, and the customs of women."—*Philadelphia Inquirer.*

THE PYGMIES. By A. DE QUATREFAGES, late Professor of Anthropology at the Museum of Natural History, Paris. With numerous Illustrations. 12mo. Cloth, $1.75.

"Probably no one was better equipped to illustrate the general subject than Quatrefages. While constantly occupied upon the anatomical and osseous phases of his subject, he was none the less well acquainted with what literature and history had to say concerning the pygmies. . . . This book ought to be in every divinity school in which man as well as God is studied, and from which missionaries go out to convert the human being of reality and not the man of rhetoric and text-books."—*Boston Literary World.*

THE BEGINNINGS OF WRITING. By W. J. HOFFMAN, M. D. With numerous Illustrations. 12mo. Cloth, $1.75.

"The author, as one of the foremost of our ethnologists, is well qualified for the inquiry, and the result of his labors is not only a monument to his industry, but a most valuable contribution to our national history as well. It is a book full of interest even to the general reader, while to the scientist it is a rich mine of facts."—*Chicago Evening Post.*

IN PREPARATION.

THE SOUTH SEA ISLANDERS. By Dr. SCHMELTZ.
THE ZUÑI. By FRANK HAMILTON CUSHING.
THE AZTECS. By Mrs. ZELIA NUTTALL.

D. APPLETON AND COMPANY, NEW YORK.

D. APPLETON & CO.'S PUBLICATIONS.

WEALTH AND PROGRESS. A Critical Examination of the Labor Problem. The Natural Basis for Industrial Reform, or How to Increase Wages without Reducing Profits or Lowering Rents : the Economic Philosophy of the Eight-Hour Movement. By GEORGE GUNTON. 12mo. Paper, 50 cents ; cloth, $1.00.

" The reader will find a statement of the labor problem as founded upon the eternal principles that underlie and the laws which govern human progress, not only through the wages system, where eight hours are practicable and feasible, but the laws which govern social evolution in all its stages, from savagery to the highest phases of civilization. '—*Christian at Work.*

SPEECHES AND ADDRESSES OF WILLIAM McKINLEY. From his Election to Congress to the Present Time. Compiled by JOSEPH P. SMITH. With Portraits on Steel of the Author and Others. 8vo, 650 pages. Cloth, $2.00.

These selections, sixty-five in number, embrace a wide range of topics of absorbing public interest, and include twenty-five speeches devoted to the tariff question in all its aspects, and others on silver, Federal elections, pensions, and the public debt, civil-service reform, the Treasury surplus and the purchase of bonds, the direct tax bill, etc. The orator whose views are thus presented is the best authority of his party on most of the matters considered. An elaborate analytical Index gives the volume an encyclopedic character, which will be especially appreciated at the present time by the student of whatever political faith.

NATURAL RESOURCES OF THE UNITED STATES. By JACOB HARRIS PATTON, A. M., Ph. D., author of " Four Hundred Years of American History," etc. Revised, with Additions. 8vo. Cloth, gilt top, $3.00.

" Covers everything, from the rarest minerals to seedless oranges. . . . A most comprehensive volume "—*Philadelphia Press.*

" A valuable summary of our native wealth. It treats not only of the precious metals, coal, iron, and petroleum, but of natural gas, building stones, fire clay, kaolin, abrasive materials, mineral springs, salt deposits. grasses, orchard fruits, deposits of gypsum, marl and phosphate, wild game, and fur-bearing animals. There are chapters on irrigation, health resorts, resources in water power and in lands. The section on our fisheries is deeply interesting, and contributes fresh scenes to the general panorama of our national prosperity. . . . No reader of this work can consistently despair of the future of the great republic."—*Philadelphia Ledger.*

STUDIES IN MODERN SOCIALISM AND LABOR PROBLEMS. By T. EDWIN BROWN, D. D. 12mo. Cloth, $1.25.

" This volume by Dr. Brown is one of the best books on the subject. It should be studied by all, in order that any discussion of it, whether in the pulpit or in private conversation, should be intelligent."—*Cincinnati Christian Advocate.*

New York : D. APPLETON & CO., 72 Fifth Avenue.

D. APPLETON & CO.'S PUBLICATIONS.

CHAPTERS IN POLITICAL ECONOMY. By Albert S. Bolles, Lecturer on Political Economy in the Boston University. Square 12mo. Cloth, $1.50.

Contents.—The Field and Importance of Political Economy; The Payment of Labor; On the Increase of Wages; Effect of Machinery on Labor; On the Meaning and Causes of Value; A Measure of Value; Money and its Uses; Decline in the Value of Gold and Silver; The Money of the Future; The Good and Evil of Banking; The Financial Panic of 1873; Relation of Banks to Speculators; Influence of Credit on Prices; On Legal Interference with the Loan of Money, Payment of Labor, and Contracts of Corporations; Advantages of Exchange; Taxation.

PROTECTION VERSUS FREE TRADE. The Scientific Validity and Economic Operation of Defensive Duties in the United States. By Henry M. Hoyt. 12mo. Cloth, $2.00; paper, 50 cents.

The author of this work is well known as formerly Governor of Pennsylvania. He appears in this volume as a defender of protection, discussing the subject in a judicial spirit, with great fullness.

PROTECTION TO HOME INDUSTRY. Four Lectures delivered in Harvard University, January, 1885. By R. E. Thompson, A. M., Professor in the University of Pennsylvania. 8vo. Cloth, $1.00.

"In these lectures Professor Thompson has stated the essential arguments for protection so clearly and compactly that it is not strange that they have produced a deep impression. . . . The lectures as printed form a neat volume, which all fairly informed students may read with interest."—*Philadelphia Item.*

TALKS ABOUT LABOR, and concerning the Evolution of Justice between Laborers and Capitalists. By J. N. Larned. 12mo. Cloth, $1.50.

The author's aim has been to find the direction in which one may hopefully look for some more harmonious and more satisfactory conjunction of capital with labor than prevails in our present social state, by finding in what direction the rules of ethics and the laws of political economy tend together.

HANDBOOK OF SOCIAL ECONOMY; or, The Worker's A B C. By Edmond About. 12mo. Cloth, $2.00.

Contents.—Man's Wants; Useful Things; Production; Parasites; Exchange; Liberty; Money; Wages; Savings and Capital; Strikes; Co-operation; Assurance, and some other Desirable Novelties.

New York: D. APPLETON & CO., 72 Fifth Avenue.

www.ingramcontent.com/pod-product-compliance
Lightning Source LLC
Chambersburg PA
CBHW021727220426
43662CB00008B/744